The Silent Trust

Life Story of Dr. Sandor Mihaly

Martin Olson

authorHOUSE®

AuthorHouse™
1663 Liberty Drive
Bloomington, IN 47403
www.authorhouse.com
Phone: 1-800-839-8640

First published by AuthorHouse   03/02/2011

ISBN: 978-1-4567-3159-5 (sc)
ISBN: 978-1-4567-3158-8 (hc)
ISBN: 978-1-4567-3157-1 (e-b)

Library of Congress Control Number: 2011901875

Printed in the United States of America

Any people depicted in stock imagery provided by Thinkstock are models, and such images are being used for illustrative purposes only. Certain stock imagery © Thinkstock.

This book is printed on acid-free paper.

SILENT TRUST

"What a strange power there is in *silence*. How many resolutions are formed, how many sublime conquests effected, during that pause when lips are closed, and the soul secretly feels the eye of the maker upon her! They are the strong ones of earth who know how to keep silence when it is a pain and grief unto them, and who give time to their own souls to wax strong against temptations."   *Emerson*

Put not your trust in money, but put your money in a *trust*.
Chinese proverb

TABLE OF CONTENTS

PROLOGUE

The Silent Trust

The Silent Trust is a true story of the power of money, and the power to keep the citizens of this world uninformed as to how the world really works in this current day and age. The true key to the success of the power brokers is just what the title implies: Secrecy.

Although I have been privy to one of the world's greatest monetary trusts, called by the simplistic designation The Swiss Trust, and have been an executive and a representative of that trust for more than a generation, dealing with European, Asian, and American governments and their political leaders, the time has come for the secrecy inherent in such trusts to be exposed to public scrutiny. Why? Because the greed that has been the motivating factor for these trusts is destroying the world in which we live.

My name is Martin Olson. Over the past several years, I have wrestled with the prospect of writing this story for fear of the imminent reprisal that would threaten my life should the truths contained herein be made public. I am presently 84 years old and I cannot idly stand-by and continue to watch the behavior of our politicians, as well as those in foreign countries, take total control of every asset that hard-working people have devoted their lives to obtain. These politicos, who have maneuvered themselves into positions of authority in governments, many times by unscrupulous or illegal means, do not care about anyone, not even those in their own constituency, or anything, except what they can gain for themselves. In our own United States, Congressmen and women are in jobs that are paid for by the taxpayers, and allot them benefits beyond any but the most wealthy in our country can afford. They are given full lifetime health and retirement pensions for the small amount of time they are actually in session, yet they are not satisfied unless they receive big gifts from large corporations or individuals.

In my dealings, I witnessed numerous acts in which people were the recipients of pay-offs that were given in return for favors that went against the professional, legal, and ethical requirements of the occupation for which they were hired. Over the period of my employment as a design engineer for Sears, and my work with the Central Intelligence Agency, the United Nations, and my being the First Business Secretary to the Chairman of the Swiss Trust, I have been given insight into activities that most people would not believe exist.

Some prime examples of what takes place in Washington, DC and around the world, will be shown in the following pages, as I open the books and notes and memos on all the missions that I have taken for years, beginning with President Richard Nixon and going forward to today. This book contains facts, and those facts are supplemented with photocopies of governmental as well as private papers that are irrefutable evidentiary proof of what encompasses the allegations made in this book.

INTRODUCTION

It was 1982 and I am about to return to Khartum, Sudan, to try to arrange financing for a closed textile mill in the city. Due to the fact that I was to be in the Sudan at a very dangerous time, although I was not made aware of it, I was working with a CIA operative out of Miami, Florida. I had fully believed that the CIA was providing me with one of their agents because I had worked with them previously in Cyprus and Hungary on projects where they traveled with me *in cognito* and appeared to be part of a design tem for hydro-electric dams. In actuality, they were using me as a means by which to take photographs and acquire names of government officials. While I was *en route*, I received a call from a friend in Washington, D.C., who was an officer of the World Bank, the institution that was responsible for my visit to Khartum. He informed me that I should call a man in New York who is head of the largest private trust in the world. He was staying at the Statler Hilton Hotel. I called and arranged a meeting at the hotel, which would be on my way to Sudan. I met with him and his wife and explained my background and what I knew of the details of the textile mill in Sudan. It was then that I discovered that he was the person who was interested in financing this mill through the World Bank. He agreed to look at the proposal I had formulated but he also asked me to talk to the Minister of Petroleum about the purchase of their oil refinery located on the Red Sea, as it was his understanding that it might be for sale. I agreed and left for Sudan.

I met with the Minister of Petroleum and I found that they only wanted to sell their product, and had no interest in disposing of their refinery. I also met with their Minister of Finance, who told me that they wanted to borrow five-hundred million U.S. dollars over a five year period and, as a result, they gave me a proposal to take back to New York.

While I was in Khartum visiting with the government officials, they asked me to meet with the group that had arranged the murder of President Anwar Sadat or Egypt in 1981. After that meeting, they asked that I have dinner with the general who was the director of the terrorist training camp in Sudan. This is the camp in which Osama Bib Laden was trained. After that meeting, I reported back to the CIA about the meetings and asked what I should do? The reply was, "Forget it. They're only a bunch of camel riders." So, I ended any further meetings. Sounds just like the CIA, with no one on the inside who knows what is really going on.

This was the time that Islam came out of the box after centuries of suppression of being held down. They will never go back into the box, as they have now had the taste of power. The Iraqi's two wars opened a whole new world for Islam.

I also met with the Minister of the Interior and discussed many needed projects in Sudan. After about a two-week stay, I was told by the Minister of the Interior that a coup was about to happen by the military within the next seven days and that I should leave immediately. I left the next day for New York.

I gave a detailed report to the Chairman of the Trust. He then informed me that he accepted my report and then asked me to work with him as his personal assistant with access to his projects and, eventually, to all aspects of the Swiss Trust, which for this report will be used, interchangeably, with the term Silent Trust. He wanted to 're-tool' me to think and act as a Swiss. I would be his assistant in international projects. This started my 15-year journey as the second in command to Dr. Sandor Mihaly, the Chairman of the largest private trust in the world.

On the pages that follow will be the true story of Dr. Mihaly's life, which is limited to his work as a scientist and the head of the Silent Trust, as I do not know much about his younger years, or his parents and family. His father was the previous Chairman of the Swiss Silent Trust and died during WWII; and his sister was a nuclear physicist in Russia. The Doctor's very talented wife was a doctor in the scientific field of gastroenterology.

Martin Olson

ABOUT THE AUTHOR...

My name is Martin Olson. By trade I am a builder, real estate developer and planner. I am an American in every aspect of the meaning of that word. I guess that is what bothers me. I always took as Gospel everything that our government said because I have always trusted the people we have elected to office fully believing that they have been the best people for the job of representing what America stands for. Throughout history, I have been proud of the choices our citizens have made in all aspects of the leaders for our nation. Granted there have been a few who have been more self-serving than the others but by and large the overwhelming majority have been good guys – the best of the best. Or, so I thought.

Never would I have even considered that anyone with such authority and power would withhold information from the American people unless it was during a time of war and secrecy was a necessity. Otherwise, we as Americans are entitled to know what is going on with our elected officials. I mean, after all, we are the people who gave these candidates their position of trust. Further, they knew that whomever the candidates chose to run the various areas of government, like them, would be people of the utmost integrity, loyal to our country and the American way of life.

When allegations were made back in the 1940's that a weather balloon fell to earth in Roswell, New Mexico, with crash dummies, rather than a saucer-like space craft with real aliens on board, naturally I believed, as did most Americans, what I was told through the media as they reported what they were told by our trustworthy government officials. Initial reports were dismissed as Orson Welles fiction.

When President John F. Kennedy was assassinated by Lee Harvey Oswald, it was determined that he acted alone, even though he fired three shots in quick succession all from a bolt-action rifle that required a minute amount of time to re-cock, and all the bullets found their mark. The allegations, however, indicated more than one perpetrator had been involved by virtue of the fact that the Zabruder film of the President's head wounds showed him jerking in two different directions when each shot was fired. Yet, according to the Warren Commission, a thorough examination proved that there was no collusion with any other person, faction, or group. As a good American I believed what I read.

When President Richard M. Nixon stood before the American people during a televised interview and stated unequivocally that he had no knowledge of what transpired, or who was behind the break-in, at the Watergate Hotel, we believed him because he was our President. He brought our soldiers back from Vietnam to stop the taking of American lives and we trusted him. How could he be expected to know anything of what had taken place at the Watergate?

It was not until I was confronted by members of the United States Secret Service, the White House, the United States Treasury and the State Department who threatened me with non-existence if I did not cooperate with their demands over an issue that had been buried for years that I finally began to see something I would never have thought to be real – that our government will resort to whatever means necessary to keep certain things secret from the American people. As a major developer with one of the country's largest corporations I had dealt with such people as Clark Clifford and other high-ranking government officials as well as governors, mayors and prime motivators of national, state and city administrations, but these people were small potatoes compared to those whom I discovered were actually in control of our country.

In 1991, I unintentionally discovered records, when I was acting as a courier for a monetary trust in Switzerland and the United States, that would bring great embarrassment to our country and its leaders. At that time I did not realize just how devastating the information they held might be to those in power in our country. In an effort to search out the basis for what I found, and while trying to accomplish a mission I had been employed to complete, I evidently stepped into something that, if exposed, would be volatile. It was at that point in time my daughter was told that, if I continued in my probe and did not cooperate fully by dong what I was told, my life would no longer have any worth. As though to emphasize their threat they also told her that her children would be taken away from her permanently. What they hinted at was that our entire family would not be in existence as it once was. They frightened her enough so that she fully believed what she was being told.

What you are about to read is true. I am now at an age where I do not care what may happen to me. The chairman of the monetary trust in Switzerland and the United States, before his death, had given me his approval to write this story. Some people will say that this is all a lie. Well, in time, and with the passing away of most of the players in this story, that will become easier to swallow than the truth. Still, I have principles that demand I can do nothing else but tell what I know and to let the chips fall where they may.

Currently, I am in excellent health for my age. However, if something unexpected or untoward should happen to me, perhaps you, as the reader, will believe what I have come to know. If I am allowed to complete my life without incident, then the choice will be up to you to decide if this was factual or just a figment of my imagination, as the government would have you believe.

In writing this book, I felt that I needed to give the reader a bit of an overview of my life, first. This is followed by a quick look at how I came to be a part of this story. I began my journey through life in East Haven, Connecticut in 1926. My actual training started in 1945 when I worked as a tracer for Snow & Nasbeth, a drafting and engineering firm in New Haven that specialized in making war products. What is a tracer? They do not exist any more. Remember, this was the 1940's when there were no modern copying devices, no such thing as a photocopy machine or anything as advanced as a computer aided drawing. So, when an engineer sent down plans for the drafting department for a new project, it was my job to trace those designs, using ink and not pencil (no corrections allowed – it had to be perfect from the inception), so that they could be submitted to the manufacturer. Because I was rated 4F when I registered for the draft, I was told to look for work in a defense-related plant, hence my position with Snow & Nasbeth. I remained with that company for two years before I went to work as a draftsman for Henry Kelly, a professor at Yale Architecture School, which really taught me to design and develop buildings versus devices. I stayed in his employ for three years before I joined the family business of designing and erecting strip malls in New England. Although my father had some insight into good locations to invest in these new after-war malls, he was not a builder. Any area that looked like it had some potential found him working deals with contractors to build these structures. So, when I came to work for him, I took the job of building contractor. I looked at the requests of the tenant, arranged financing for the project, drafted and designed the structures, and pulled together the team that would fulfill every aspect of the project. I always knew who was doing what and my father never had to worry about anything. The end result was that I made a lot of money for my father during those years from 1950 to 1959. This started my life's role as a coordinator. Our family business was responsible for building and leasing department stores, such as Sears & Roebuck, and S.S. Kresge, along with banks, supermarkets, and theaters. I concentrated especially on drafting the construction plans, obtaining the permits, and managing the construction from beginning to completion.

It might interest people to know that I learned from doing things. I had a very limited formal education. The reason being that I found school boring with a lack of any real challenge. I by-passed the basics of college and went directly into drafting after listening to a minister friend of mine who new my family quite well and once asked me if I was always going to walk the picket fence. Did I want to keep on doing what I was doing with no apparent goal, or did I want to walk on the same side as he did, with an opportunity to develop into someone of talent. I recall this Toronto, Canadian born preacher who was a circuit-rider and would travel from church to church every Sunday, but who was also a Yale professor with a great knowledge of the Bible. In my early years, he taught me how to read the Bible, how to meet people, and how to express myself in all situations. Adding all these things together, allowed me to move to the next step.

I left the family business and was employed by Sears, Roebuck and Company to manage construction and maintenance in New England. This enabled me to move to Philadelphia, the eastern territory main office, where I took over as manager of the property department. This lasted ten years.

I started my own business in Doylestown, Pennsylvania. I then was engaged by the Hilton Hotels Corporation to work for them. I later became involved doing urban renewal in downtown Detroit, Michigan and was named the successful developer in bidding to build the new IRS computer center from the Government General Services Administration. Once that was completed, I moved to Camden, Maine, and purchased the Samoset Hotel in Rockport, Maine. The building was torched, so I then put up a new convention hall with an 18-hole golf course. I opened the hotel just before the late 1970's recession. I was also chairman of the Camden Hospital new expansion program.

It was after this that I received a call from Washington, DC to meet with a CIA operative in Miami, Florida. This led to my being involved in projects in Africa, South America, the Middle East and Europe. During this period, I received a call from the World Bank, with a request that I meet the Chairman of The Swiss Trust in New York, Dr. Sandor Mihaly. This began my last journey and most important task in my life; the writing of this book, *The Silent Trust*.

My mission for Dr. Mihaly took me all over the world covering several tasks. I kept notes including memos on all the projects and missions that enable me to tell this true story. Before the doctor passed away, he wanted me to promises to tell the world the story of what happened for history in order that it not be lost or burned. His wife, Maria, who was dying a slow death from cancer, also reminded me to have this story made public. She, in fact, sent to me many documents, such as precious metal deposits, securities, and bond deposit statements, to be a part of this writing.

I wrestled with the idea of writing and publishing *The Silent Trust* for a few years, and what changed my mind was the behavior of our politicians. They do not care about anyone, except what is in it for themselves. They have a position and are paid by the taxpayers for their time, including full time health and retirement benefits and they still are not happy unless they get these big gifts from large corporations and individuals. I felt it was time to tell the true story about Richard Nixon, as an example of what really goes on behind closed doors.

As I mentioned earlier, before I sent to work for the doctor, I was property manager for Sears, Roebuck and Company, Eastern Territory, and handled the area from Boston to Washington, D.C. Those stories are not a part of this book, but they are the same story of the hunger for, and the influence of, money. As it has been stated in Washington for years, "Money talks, everything else walks." Nothing has changed except that it has gotten worse.

I worked with Attorney Clark Clifford in Washington during the 1960's. Clark was advisor to six Presidents, and was the Secretary of Defense for a short time. Clark told me that the current form of government will not last because it is top heavy with corruption. Now this was in the 1960's and it is now 50 years later and nothing has changed except for the fact that it has escalated.

This book is about facts, which will be seen as one reads and views the photocopies of documents written by several governments as well as Dr. Mihaly and his vision, which was not completed in his lifetime.

It is my hope that this book will enlighten you and maybe someone will attempt to complete the doctor's mission for an International Medical University and Institute of Bio-Medicine. My wife and I formed the Institute of Bio-Medicine, LLC, A Delaware Corporation that is currently active.

I pray that someone or group would come forth to investigate the great benefit that this medical university would give to mankind. Now that NANO-medicine is coming onto the scene, it would be a tremendous asset in the doctor's concept to provide the latest medical discoveries that would be available to the medical world free of charge.

PRESIDENCY OF THE REPUBLIC
SECRETARIAT GENERAL
OFFICE OF THE
THE MINISTER

رئاسة الجمهورية
الامانة العامة
الـــوزير

No:RP/SG/SOC/20-A-4/9/587/1405   Date : 27th.Jumadi-El-Akhra,1405
19th. March, 1985.

Mr. Martin Olson,
     President,
       Sodesa Co. Ltd U.S.A.

      During the recent meetings you have had with the representatives of the Bank of Sudan on the subject of a cash loan of U.S.$500 million offered by your institutions we are pleased to convey our approval in principle to the following terms and conditions mutually agreed upon:

1.   Amount:

      U.S.$500,000,000 to be disbursed as follows:
      1)   U.S.$200,000,000 upon closing of documents
      2)   U.S.$125,000,000 3 months from closing
      3)   U.S.$125,000,000 6 months from closing
      4)   U.S.$50,000,000 9 months from closing

2.   Repayment:

      1)   U.S.$200,000,000 $5\frac{1}{2}$ years from closing
      2)   U.S.$125,000,000 6 years from transfer
      3)   U.S.$125,000,000 $6\frac{1}{2}$ years from transfer
      4)   U.S.$50,000,000 7 years from transfer

3.   Interest 8%per annum with 2years grace.

THE DEMOCRATIC REPUBLIC OF THE SUDAN

PRESIDENCY OF THE REPUBLIC

SECRETARIAT GENERAL

OFFICE OF THE

THE MINISTER

جمهورية السودان الديمقراطية

رئاسة الجمهورية

الامانة العامة

الوزير

-2-

In order to finalize this offer and conclude the relevant legal documents it is a precondition that Bank of Sudan receives a tested telex message from a prime bank confirming availability of funds as to the extent of the total loan refered to above within seven days from the date of this letter. I would like to confirm that if the tested telex is not received within the specified period we consider the offer as null and void.

Mohamed El Hassan Ahmed El Hag,
Minister For Presidential Affairs &
Rapporteur of the Supreme Council
For National Economy

C.C./ H.E Farouk I. Magboul,
Governor, Central Bank
of Sudan.

CRUDE OIL CONTRACT

This CONTRACT is signed and entered into at Khartoum
Sudan on the 6.23.14... duped at that in the year 1405H,
equivalent to OST 5.14... day of March in the year 1985 between:-

SODESA CO., LTD., U.S.A.
Presented by Martin Olson, President

A N D

GENERAL PETROLEUM CORPORATION
P.O. Box 2986
Presented by Dr. Omer el Shaikh Omer

ARTICLE 1 :   Quantity: 100,000 MTPS per month for total
              period of 36 months. Each monthly order to
              be delivered in two lots of 50,000 MT/each.

ARTICLE 2 :   Quality : Arabian light crude oil API 34.

ARTICLE 3 :   Delivery : Within 30 days of acceptance of
              this CONTRACT and financed by the finance
              lender of SODESA CO. LTD.

ARTICLE 4 :   Price : 28.00 CIF Port Sudan. This is sub-
              ject to 3 x 3 x 3 month evergreen clause,
              normal wording used in Crude Oil Contracts and
              to any extensions addendum, or renewals. This
              price is based on the official Arabian light
              API 34 prevailing on the date of signature of

                                                    2/2.

this Contract plus floating interest rate
adjustable every three months, as used in
typical clauses using Citibank, New York,
U.S.A. as a base of any increase or decr-
ease of interest rates?

ARTICLE 5: Payment: by confirmed irrevocable letter
of credit covering 3 months supplies with
partial shipment allowed? Available by
beneficiaries 360 days days(s) from date
of B/L including floating interest charge
payable on actual cost subject to article
4? Lenders are fully responsible to secure the prior approval of the confirming
bank and/ OR banks?

ARTICLE 6: Insurance : If any policies of insurance,
not including cargo insurance, that the lender inquires, as part of this financing Contract, to be an additional charge and charged
by lender and approved by buyer?

ARTICLE 7: Demurrage: Lay time after 36 hours + 6 hours
N.O.R. Time shall count for demurrage?

ARTICLE 8: Inspection: Quantity & quality will determined
at loading and discharging ports by independent
inspector, binding final for both parties?

ARTICLE 9: Other terms & Conditions: Other terms and conditions as per normal for this type of transaction add as per oil industry parties , including
force majeur clause normally used?

3/4.7

ARTICLE 10: Increases: Buyer has right to increase
tonnage of crude within 30 days notice.
In the event buyer's refinery shuts down,
a 60 day notice, to be given to seller so
as to replace crude oil with equivalent
quantity of refined oil. Price to be agreed upon accordingly.

ARTICLE 11: Financing: This Contract is subject to
approval of Sedena Co. Ltd. financial lender and central bank gurantee given to lender. This Contract is to be validated within
7 working days from the date of singature
supported by key tested telex and preeadvise
from bank nominated by lenders communicating
their prior approval to add their confimation
to the respective letter (s) of credit.

On Behalf Of   On Behalf Of

MR. MARTIN OSLOW   DR. OMER EL SHEIKH OMER

BODESA CO. LTD   CENTRAL PETROLEUM CORPO...
                             15 ... 1985
                             GENERAL MANAGER OFFICE

AGM HOLDING CORPORATION
(Wilmington, Delaware)

Mr.Martin Olson
identified by Passprot,
attached the copy to
the file of AGM.

No.381753-220/1

New York,Apr.6,1985.

Mailing address:
114 OLD COUNTRY RD
MINEOLA, NEW YORK 11501
(516) 746 1870

It is hereby confirmed with full Corporate Responsibility,that AGM Holding
Corp. will pay consultant fee to you under terms,conditions as follows:

1.
Subject:crude oil,from Saudi Arabia ,up to one million barrels per day 3x3 year
contracts,as to regular contracts,payable fee to you: US Dollars 0.01125 (equal
1.125 cent per barrel).
2.
To be used the Central Bank of Sudan as passthrough banking mechanism and the
oil company and refinery(ies) owned or controlled by the Gvmnt of Sudan.
3.
AGM shall be the trustee,agent or fully authorized representative of the entities,listed in par.no.2.
4.
Contract shall be signed between the Saudies and AGM in ref. to above paragraphs.
5.
All negotiations and arrangements for the preparation of the contracts to be
done by Dr.Bilal,Mr.Olsen and Mr.Hodges as to directions by AGM.
6.
Cotton related brokerage also subject to these commitment,however the payable
consultant fee shall be determined upon availability of all date,and shall
be issued   separate commitments.
7.
At these stage AGM waive any responsibilites regarding any fees,expenses,front
payments,whatsoever nature.As soon as the deal is working,AGM will provide proper
arrangements for expenses.
8.
These commitment is legally binding,however expires within 60 days from today
data,if will not be possible to make any progress,which shows that the deal is
working.
In other case,AGM shall renew these commitment,automatically issuing a new document with the same basic conditions,with detailed banking arrangements.

THIS COMMITMENT IS NOT FINANCIAL INSTRUMENT AND IT IS NON TRANSFERABLE AND CANNOT
BE USED AS COLLATERAL OR FOR ANY FINANCIAL PURPOSES WHATSOEVER.

Dr.Maria Mihaly,Peterfi
Co-Chairman of AGM Holdings

Dr Sandor Mihaly
Chairman of AGM Holdings

AGM HOLDING CORPORATION
(Wilmington, Delaware)

No.381753-262

Mailing address:
114 OLD COUNTRY RD.
MINEOLA, NEW YORK 11501
(516) 746-1870
or:
PO Box 10085
Riviera Beach
Fla 33404
(305)845-8122

Mr.Martin G.Olson
24 Jupiter Dr.
New Port Richey
Florida 33552

Dear Mr. Olson:

As per our recent verbal authorization you are hereby authorized to negotiate on behalf of our Holdings the purchase of Oil Refineries and/or oil
products trading companies.

All financial data shall be requested for evaluation,before will be decided to enter into direct negotiation in merit.Your arrangement has the purpose to clearify the basic financial and technical parameters and present
all essential data to the Chairman for evaluation,including your reccommen-
dations.

It is imperativ to understand,that no middle organization can be involved into
this deal and no brokerage fee will be paid to any one.Any kind of speculative
element will be eliminated in once upon discover it.

Shall be explained to the other parties that AGM at this stage do not disclose
any financial capabilities however in proper time will be provided precise
banking and financial information whereby the necessary funds will be confirmed.

This authorization cannot be disclosed to any third parties without the
writte consent of the Chairman.Any deviation from these guidance may result
serious consequences and withraw of intent to purchase.

Mr. Olsen in case of request,may sign on behalf of AGM a non disclosure
agreement.

This authorization give no authority to Mr. Olson to make any commitments,pro-
mises,whatsoever financial nature concerning the subject;all decision shall be
made only after evaluation of the satisfactory data to be furnished by the
other party.

--2--

Mr. Olson acts on behalf of AGM Holdings and his compenzation to be considered as internal matter of AGM Holdings.

It is understood that this authorization is in accordance with the decision of the Board of Directors of AGM and expires upon completed deals, but not later than Sep.1,1985.

Sincerely:

Dr.Sandor Mihaly,Chairman
Chief Operating Officer of AGM.

AGM HOLDING CORPORATION
(Wilmington, Delaware)

No.381753-264

Mailing address:
114 OLD COUNTRY RD.
MINEOLA, NEW YORK 11501
(516) 746-1870

W Palm Beach,July 22,1985.

Mr.Martin Olson
24 Jupiter Dr.
New Port Richey
Florida 33552

Dear Mr. Olson:

This letter confirms our personal discussions regarding the planned new
department of AGM,under a new,wholy owned subsidiary,concerning the crude
oil deal,recently analyzed.

AGM has access to very substantial crude oil and AGM plans to sign processing
agreements with various refineries and shiping companies in order to obtain
refined products and to sale them.

For the realization of this plan would be necessary to set up a unified
department,which will be bussy only with the shiping problems,due to the
substantial amount of crude and refined products in question.

For the shiping department AGM looking for an experiences person,and the appointed person will be named as maning director of the subsidiary.(Shiping untl).
Of course,the compensation of the appointed person,after proper examination
and passing various tests,will be in accordance with the practice in USA
in the same field.Mostly this type of executives having yearly salary and
additional substantial premium which is related with the amount of US Dls as
volume or as revenue will be handled per year by the same managing director.

There are various listings,appeared in the Forbes or Fortune known magazins,
whereby in the various industries the full compenzation are listed.In the above
mentioned case,whereby the handled crude would be very substantial,the referred
managing director mostly having the category USD 70 000 up to USD 200 000 per
year,plus premium.
At this stage is very difficoult to estimate the figures,since the crude related contract not yet in hand of AGM and therefore cannot be provided any responsible promise in this subject,however the probability is very substantial that
crude will be under jurisdiction of AGM within relatively short period of
time.The OPEC related problems interfare,time wise,however seems to be very ma-
ture the situation AGM point of views.

-2-

AGM HOLDING CORPORATION
(Wilmington, Delaware)

Mailing address:
114 OLD COUNTRY RD.
MINEOLA, NEW YORK 11501
(516) 746-1870

As soon as the contract in hands of AGM,immediately will be selected the chief staff for the whole crude business and among others also Mr. Olson is to be considered very seriously as such person who will pass all necessary tests during the examination.

If Mr. Olson- we assume that he will - will be qualified,passing the various tests,we will propose to the Board of Directors,to nominate as managing director of the shipling subsidiary with substantial poer and of course responsibility, consequently with substantial yearly slary and premiums,benefits in range of executives as indicated above.

Dear Mr. Olson,this letter has been issued for your request and we hope really, that you will be able to comply with all requirements and very soon could be discussed the five years contract as managing director and executive officer of AGM.

This letter of course cannot be considered as promise or any obligation from side of AGM,purely and informative one and since our evaluation and opinion about your ability more and more became positive,therefore we will provide supportive opinion about your personality and ability.

Time wise,without any obligation- within few weeks shall be decided about this matter,because the crude contract will be in our hands very soon.

We hope and believe,that you are the right person for the above described job and therefore we support you nomination.

You will be adviced soon about the next step to be taken in this subject.

Sincerely

Dr.Sandor Mihaly,Chairman,AGM.

WE ARE SRRY ABOUT TYPING EROODS.

COMPLEX INDUSTRIES HOLDINGS LTD.

P.O.BOX 15288 WEST PALM BEACH
FLORIDA 33416-5288
TEL:(305) 844-3218
FAX: (305) 845-1261
TLX: 5106016718 EUROINVEST

FRED.S.JAMES & CO.OF FL,INC.
1555 PALM BEACH LAKES BLVD.
SUITE 800
WEST PALM BEACH,FL,33401   Aug.18,1987.

Gentlemen:

It is hereby confirmed,that

                    MR.MARTION OLSON,Director,
                    First Business Secretary to
                        the Chairman

is fully authorized to negotiate all matters on behalf of Complex
Industries Holdings Ltd.

Final contracts,documents to be approved and signed by Dr.Sandor
Mihaly,Chairman.
This authorization expires on Dec 31,1987.

Sincerely Yours:

Dr.Sandor Mihaly.
   Chairman
 CI Holdings.

CHAPTER ONE

The Making of a Scientist

Sandor Mihaly was born on February 28, 1925 in Dunakeszi, in the region of Pest, Hungary (part of Budapest). As a young man, he entered into the Second World War from the Hungarian side and was part of the Hungarian Intelligence Department and worked in Hungary decoding the German enigmatic codes. This was at a time when Gene Casey was at the held of the United States Intelligence Service and was later to head the Central Intelligence Agency in the 1960's and 1970's.

Completing his military service, Sandor Mihaly entered Jozsef Attica University of Sciences where he studied between the years 1949 to 1950 and 1952 to 1963. He had further studies in Austria at Wien at the University of Engineering and Telecommunications from the first term of 1955 to 1956, and a second session in 1963 to 1964. This university is a counterpart to the Massachusetts Institute of Technology.

The first of the Doctor's degrees was as a pathologist. Dr. Mihaly also received his degree in Electronic Engineering on March 5, 1966. He also received his doctorate in Natural Sciences with honors on July 13, 1963. The Doctor received his certificate as a Patent Attorney on January 17, 1968. He received a license to practice industrial installation of freeze-drying, vacuum instruments and accessories on April 11, 1968.

Dr. Sandor Mihaly had made 75 medical discoveries that he had patented, which he turned over to the Silent Swiss Trust in exchange for full payment of his yearly living expenses. Two of the discoveries were: the first birth control pill, and the first process for freeze-dried products.

The Doctor discovered the first birth control pill in Europe, which was copied and drastically changed for the American market. The Doctor warned the companies in the United States that the change could cause cancer, which, in the end, proved out. The pill was then taken off of pharmacy shelves.

The Doctor later discovered the freeze-dry system of processing foods. This was copied by the Nestle Company that started freeze-drying coffee as a part of its commodities.

After his father's death during the Second World War, Dr. Mihaly was asked by the Swiss Silent Trust to take over his father's position. Once in that new role, he embarked upon a study to utilize the Trust assets to better mankind with such projects as hospitals, clinics, research laboratories, and medical universities, which would be paid for by taking the assets of the Trust and the collateral formula to raise capital and still keep the Trust's assets in a safe position. All of this was to come with guarantees by the various governments in which the projects were to be developed. This, likewise, included plans for transportation, petroleum, and petro-chemical undertakings, housing, and utility activities, but nothing that would involve the military.

The Doctor was invited by the U.S. Government to move to the United States in 1960, where he became a citizen in 1968. He became a member of the Republican Eagles and was a supporter of the Republican Party. Oh, to have friends in high places. The United States asked that he bring the Trust business with him. *Why not!*

During the 1980's, the Doctor had a special agreement with NATO Headquarters in Ramstein, Germany, under General Haig and General Lustig to organize specialized health facilities. After General Haig's retirement, he kept close with Dr. Mihaly at the General's secondary residence in Palm Beach, Florida where he often visited the area for certain conferences for business organizations.

Dr. Sandor Mihaly

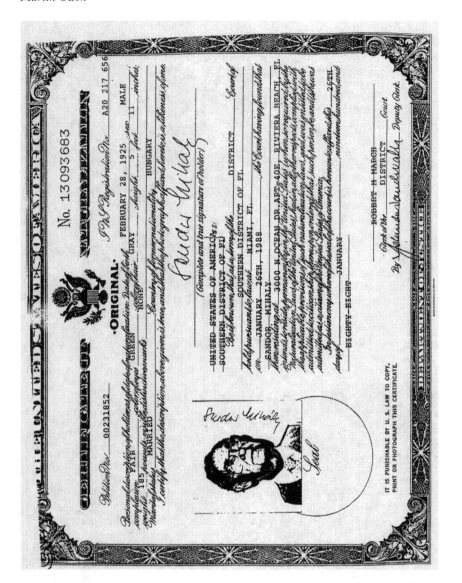

Dr. Sandor Mihaly – the middle years

Maria and Sandor Mihaly – the later years

CHAPTER TWO

The Swiss Silent Trust

Some background...

Dr. Sandor Mihaly's background shows that he is a descendant of royalty. His family was a part of the Hungarian monarchy. His relatives include, Mihaly Karoly, who was Premier of Hungary from 1918 to 1919, when he became President of the country.

There exist two public squares in Pest, that part of Budapest where Sandor was born. Mihaly Vorosmarty Square is named for a poet whose monument, depicting him, is erected in the middle of the square. It is inscribed with his dates of living from 1800 to 1855 and was unveiled in 1908.

Mihaly Pollack Square is at the rear of the Hungarian National Museum and is named for the architect of several neoclassical buildings such as the museum and Sandor Palace, which is now occupied by the President of Hungary.

Hungary has in its history a long number of conflicts since the year 14 B.C. Now, it is a member of NATO. Back in those early years, Western Hungary was a part of the Roman Empire, whereas the area to the east of the Danube River was not. In 896 A.D., all of Hungary was invaded by the Magyars. Christianity was accepted during the reign of St. Stephen from 977 to 1038 A.D. An Invasion by the Mongols killed half of Hungary's population in 1241 A.D. The peak of the Hungarian great period of power came during the reign of Louis I, the Great, between 1342 and 1382 A.D. In 1839, war broke out with the Turks and, for more than a hundred years, the Turks advanced through the Balkans. The Turks smashed the Hungarian Army in 1526, while Western and Northern Hungary accepted Hapsburg Rule to escape the Turkish occupation. Transylvania, which had previously been a province of Hungary, became an independent entity under the Hungarian monarchy. A peace treaty was signed in 1699. After the suppression of the 1848 revolt against Hapsburg Rule, led by Louis Kossuth, a dual monarchy of Austria-Hungary was set up in 1867. The dual monarchy was defeated with other central powers in World War I. After a short-lived republic in 1918, the Communist rule of 1919 under Dela Kon ended with the Romanian occupation of Budapest in August of 1919.

The Treaty of Trianon in 1920 cost Hungary 68% of its land and 58% of its population. The Hungarian Monarchy had restored the legal continuity of the old monarchy and, in 1920, Horthy was elected Regent. Following the German invasion of Russia in 1941, Hungary joined the attack against Russia and the Hungarian troops were almost entirely withdrawn from the eastern front in 1943. The German occupation troops set up a puppet government after Horthy's appeal for an armistice with the advanced Russian troops in 1944, which resulted in Horthy's being overthrown. The German regime soon fled the capitol. In 1945, the government signed an armistice in Moscow, and in 1946, the National Assembly approved a constitutional law abolishing the 1000-year monarchy and establishing a republic.

"Budapest was the site of one of the fiercest battles of World War II. Stalin and Hitler demanded a victory at all costs. This battle took place between December 29, 1944 and February 11, 1945, a total of 100 days. The cost of the battle for control of Budapest and Hungary was 80,000 Soviet troops, 38,000 German and Hungarian soldiers, and 38,000 Hungarian civilians. All perished. The diversion of Soviet troops to Budapest enabled the Germans to maintain their crumbling positions elsewhere in Hungary. A battle for control by two leaders, Hitler and Stalin, sitting in their offices while the army and civilians pay the price, Hungary has lost every war over the last 500 years. What a waste."

Kristian Ungvary

A treaty of Paris in 1947 required that Hungary give up all land it had acquired since 1937, and to pay out 300 million U.S. dollars in reparations to Russia, Czechoslavakia, and Yugoslavia. In 1948, the Communist Party seized control of the nation. This was followed by Hungary being proclaimed a People's Republic, a one-party state in 1949. All industry was nationalized. The land was collectively turned into state farms and was under the control of the secret police. The Communist wrath reached its height when, in 1948, a trial was held and a lie imprisonment sentence was meted out to Josef Cardinal Mindezenty, the leader of Hungary's Roman Catholic Church.

In 1956, an anti-Communist revolution broke out in Budapest. Premier Imre Nagy declared Hungary a neutral power, withdrawing from the Warsaw Treaty and appealing to the United Nations for help. Soviet troops and tanks suppressed the revolution in a bloody fight after 190,000 people fled the country. Under Kader Rule, between 1956 and 1988, Communist Hungary maintained liberal policies and Hungary became the most liberal of the Soviet block. Kader emptied prisons, reformed the secret police, and eased travel restrictions. Hungary's Communists voluntarily abandoned their power in 1989 and the constitution was amended to allow a multi-party state. The last Soviet troops left Hungary in 1991, ending almost 47 years of military presence. Hungary normalized relations with the Catholic Church in 1997. In April, 1999, Hungary became a part of NATO and also with the Czech Republic and Poland.

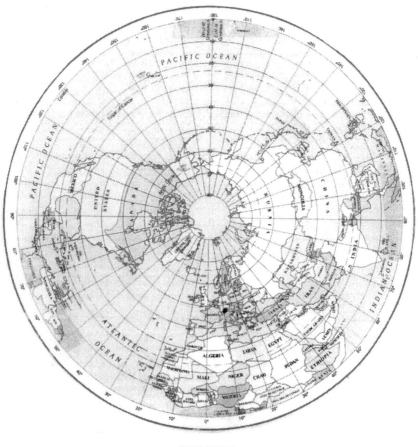

WORLD

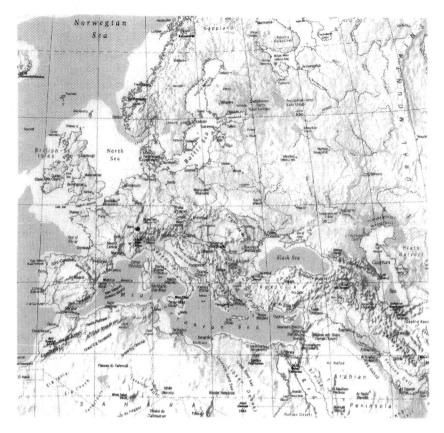

Physical map

Political map

Switzerland, Lucerne

SWITZERLAND

The silent world government meets yearly in Burgerstock, Switzerland, which lies in the northern end of Lake Lucerne. Burgerstock is next to the town of Kussnacht at the foot of Rigi. It is in the central Switzerland and Ticino District. Burgerstock has a historical castle which is owned by the Silent Trust and under Dr. Mihaly's jurisdiction.

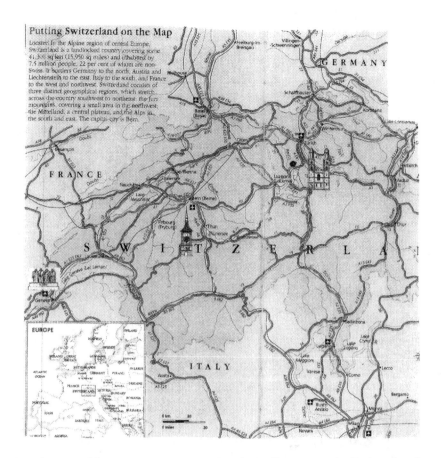

The silent world government meets yearly in Burgerstock, Switzerland, which lies in the northern end of Lake Lucerne. Burgerstock is next to the town of Kussnacht at the foot of Rigi. It is in the central Switzerland and Ticino District. Burgerstock has a historical castle which is owned by the Silent Trust and under Dr. Mihaly's jurisdiction.

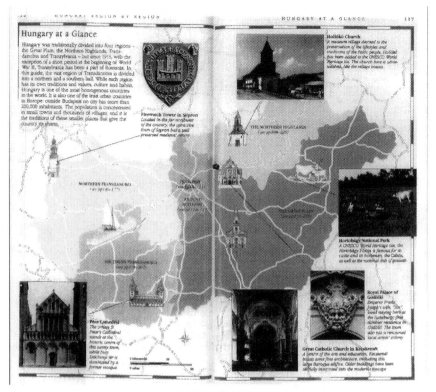

HUNGARY

Dr. Mihaly planned to locate the International Center in Godollo, Hungary. This is the site of the Godollo Royal Palace built in 1741. Godollo is located 22 miles northeast of Budapest. Godollo was established in 1661.

Now, in 2010, there is a major problem regarding the debt, which is a problem similar to that with other European and Middle-Eastern countries.

The name of the game of power is money...

Dr. Mihaly prepared a report on June 14, 1996, on the movement of world currency regarding the Silent World Government, the Bilderberg Group, and the Banks Club. It describes their meetings, members, and their mission. It also outlines the private bank, the EUBT – European Bank and Trust, which was designed and organized according to a unique trust that had been formed during the middle 1800's and was in control of many of the monetary funds deposited within its safes by numerous governmental leaders and royalty beginning from that period. Its purpose was to hold these funds, which could be used for investments by the trust, and which would produce income for the depositors. The trust was to remain secret, allowing no one access to the deposit information except for the depositors themselves. It would not be open to any government scrutiny and the depositor's names would be held in secret.

The trust knew that the name of the game of power is money. The group that controls the money has all the power. The world today is at one's fingertips with the advancement of communications beyond the telephone and television to the nano-technology of the computer. Since this is the electronic world, money can be moved instantly and globally, and most of this is currency-trading done through London and Switzerland, which operates 24-hours a day, mostly during non-banking hours. More than 80 percent of that trading is done through Switzerland.

When Dr. Sandor Mihaly took over the reigns of the trust as its Chairman during the 1950's, he continued to operate within the strictest discipline of safety for the trust's assets. Also, he never looked toward any personal gains from the trust, which seems to be opposite the workings of those who make this a practice in the world of greed. All of the business of the trust and all the details of that business were, likewise, kept in silence.

Silence and secrecy go together. With silence, one does not tell or talk; with secrecy, one does not tell or talk. With this form of silent, non-communication, one does not come under the microscope for examination by the outside world. And as long as the persons involved can keep this form, they can move freely throughout the world.

"The Nixon Administration was the high point of the 'imperial presidency, a produce of the Cold War.' Much of Nixon's foreign and military policy was concerned and executed in secrecy, outside normal administrative changes and without consultation with Congress. The power this wielded by the President, magnified by his ability to control news, and to command television time, was totally unprecedented."

American History – Robert A. Rosenbraum

The origin of the Trust...

The trust, which became the Swiss Secret Trust, is over 180 years old and was started in Switzerland. It operated at its inception as a depository for the royal families of Europe. Over generations, money and gold had been placed into the trust for safekeeping. The Queen of England had put billions in there as a nest egg in case they lost the Second World War and, thus, they could move to Switzerland and have access to the money as well as all the valuables they had stored away. Of course, they never told the citizens that.

Even Hitler had a lot of money in there before he disappeared. Should Germany have been destroyed, he would be able to continue with the wealth he had amassed.

Hungary had a lot invested because the Doctor with Hungarian. Also, Saudi Arabia, Dubai, and other wealthy Islamic countries put enormous amounts of money in there because the trust was managed by experts in currency trading. Currency trading can almost guarantee a profit of 25 percent a year, but it had to be worked 24-hours a day. That's where they made their money. All activities, monetary transactions, were carried out in England. Years ago, everything was in England, although the main center or operation was Switzerland.

Since its inception so many years ago, the Doctor never spoke very much about the trust's history. He never released information as to who were the primary movers within the trust, nor what projects the trust would finance. They theory was that the trust would only finance non-military tasks. They would not touch anything that was even remotely military. They looked mostly to hospitals and the Doctor really promoted that because he wanted to establish an international medical center. The original trust never really grew until after the Doctor's father died – it had been carried down from grandfather to father to the Doctor who re-established it as the Swiss Secret Trust.

Dr. Mihaly never told anyone how his grandfather got involved in the trust. He just said it was passed down and managed. The Doctor, after getting his medical degree from the University in Vienna, agreed to help run the trust. It was actually the Doctor who developed The Silent Trust. In fact, President Reagan became a close friend of Dr. Sandor Mihaly and invited him to come to the States and become a citizen and to bring the Trust with him. Ever since that time, every President of the United States has had to go to the Doctor to get approval to go to war. Even up to Old Man Bush going there with Kissinger. But that was then. Now, with the problems the U.S. is having with the economy, Canada is trying to bring the Trust there. I remember working with Clark Clifford in the 1960's, when I was involved in building three major malls in Washington, D.C., Clark said, in some of our discussions, the democratic system won't work, it was too corrupt. And that was in the 60's. Look at it now. It still is too corrupt. Clifford once told me, "Anything inside the Beltway is the United States; anything outside the Beltway is a disposable commodity." The people inside the Beltway control everything – the wars and everything else – they just *use* those who are outside the Beltway for their own convenience. Clark Clifford had a law office in Washington. He lived most of his life there, while his wife lived on Cape Cod.

Having been recommended to Dr. Mihaly for the position of Executive Secretary, I was once asked, "Was Dr. Mihaly, a brilliant man in every respect, as brilliant when it came to operating the Trust, or did he hire people to run the Trust where he was only the titular head?"

That was a hard question to answer. My relationship with him was for about 18 years. He had no social skills, he had a very difficult time talking with people. So, my job was to be his spokesman, whether it was with Howard Hughes, or the president of GE, or with government officials around the world. Previous to my working for the Doctor, I did this for the CIA and the United Nations. It was through these experiences that the Doctor came to know me, and to investigate me, and, finally, to ask me to go to work for him. The Doctor had some vision for the future, however, his main concern was the medical center. That was his real focus, as well as petro-chemicals because that is the basis for many medicines.

The medical facility would be a place for discovering and experimenting with new products to improve the health of the world. Foresight wise, he had me do reports constantly, and then he would read them and have me redo them three or four times. I did the ground work. For example, when it came to a new petro-chemical project, he would have me locate the work crews, the ships for transport, the location of the plant – or would we buy one, perhaps from Shell or some other company. He would do all the figures and I would do all the reports so that he could then decide whether it was worth doing, or not to go forward.

This is about what I did with Sears so many years ago because they didn't know how to build malls. I was their coordinator, in a sense, because I was the designer and builder of so many of these shopping centers, which became so popular after the 1940's, and so many malls, which became popular after the 1960's. They used me politically to get zoning and permits, because Sears didn't know how to do that. There were a number of times in those years when pay-offs had to be made to encourage people with political connections to convince local governments to re-zone properties so that Sears could build a shopping center. Sears engaged a fellow with an Armenian background to make all the pay-offs. And that's what they did, and he did it with diamonds because they are not traceable. I met this fellow a number of times and I told him that I wanted nothing to do with pay-offs; I was not going to dirty my hands with that type of negotiation. My job was in making any design changes, getting the right people, and hiring the right lawyers. That type of politics was right up my alley, the other shady stuff was not. Sears often asked me how I managed to do these things and I said it was better not to ask, just know that it was done on a handshake, no contracts, and we always kept our word – even when I dealt with the Mafia in Providence, Rhode Island, but that's another story.

The formation of the Trust...   (Edited for ease of reading and comprehension)

"The Trust operates from Switzerland, however it is established in Grenada under the British type of Secrecy Law. As reference, perhaps for the Hungarian population, it is not well-known that in Hungary there exists a very restricted Bank Secrecy and General Secrecy Law, such as that in Austria and Switzerland, and many other so-called offshore tax-haven countries in different parts of the world.

The data and records of the activity of the Trust is not subject to any public disclosure. Therefore, no information is available to anyone. The other important legislative subject is the Asset Protection Law, which prevents any lawsuit or claim from being successful against the Trust or its assets. This asset protection law exists in very few countries.

Of course, in cases of drugs, or terrorist activities, or organizations, any related monies are not protected under this law. The government has a very restrictive manner to supervise the origin of funds in order to avoid any involvement by banks in criminal businesses. This item is very important because of the number of criminal organizations, including 'Mafioso' type businesses, have been involved in money-laundering in Hungarian banks. The Trust, therefore, *per se*, is an absolutely legitimate operation, working in an anonymous manner.

It shall be understood that there is a great difference between a public and a private company or establishment.

Public companies receive funds from the public in exchange for non-voting shares. Because of the public character, that type of company or entity is regulated in a very restrictive manner in order to eliminate the possibility of fraudulent activities. For public entities, the law requires a minimum of five members on the board of directors, whereby every essential decision is subject to a vote by the five directors. Therefore, the chairman of such a type of organization has very limited power. Decisions or proposals by the chairman must be recorded in the books of the entity and may be voted down by the board of directors by a simple majority vote.

The private entities, which do not collect funds from the public, by the laws governing their action, do not have restrictions concerning the minimum number of members comprising the board of directors. One person can represent the president, secretary and treasurer, and, therefore, nominate himself or herself as chairman.

In the case of a trust, there is no board of directors. Instead, there are trustees. There can be one trustee or a number of trustees depending upon the public or private character of the trust. In the case of a private trust, there is only one trustee, and that person has unlimited and unrestricted power with unlimited responsibilities.

The Swiss Secret Trust, in this situation, has only one trustee, Dr. Sandor Mihaly. In the event of his incapacity or death, the trustee will be immediately and automatically replaced by a board of trustees (minimum of five persons). All previous decisions by the preceding trustee will remain in full force and effect as provided by the guidelines, which form the inside laws of the Trust. Therefore, the continuation of the previous decisions and business practices remain intact.

The Trust has no characteristics similar to a corporation. The Trust is not a commercial entity. It is, rather, a means for holding assets, without being a holding company. The Trust 'holds' (retains ownership of) several companies, i.e. Aktien Gesellschafts Corporation, as well as different forms of entities. The statutes of the Trust require 100 percent ownership. It does not allow any joint venture, nor partnership, in order to conserve the assets, which, by this role, is a sole ownership, and is indivisible.

Another example of such ownership is RT-s, Reszveny Tarsasag, which is 100 percent owned by the Trust.

Certain terminology needs to be explained in order to make clear who and why the owners of the Trust must remain anonymous. As an example, the aforementioned Aktien Gesellschafts entity can have registered or bearer shares. Such shares are not registered under any name. Originally, shares were issued and later converted into bearer shares, which means that the holder of the shares is the owner of the entity. There are, obviously, preventive measures in place against fraud. In every aspect, the Trust works to keep everything within its bound legitimate and morally correct.

Bearer instruments are very common in the international business fields. This can be easily seen in United States short term Treasury Bills, which have either 30, 60, or 90 day maturity. The bearer treasurer bills are the subject of daily buying and selling activities in the international money market. Since the security market operates around the clock, in every two to three minutes, on average, the treasury bills are changing ownership. That huge volume is about two trillion US dollars a day. If the treasury bills were to be registered, the related registration time requirements would make it impossible to accommodate the rapid ownership changes.

The above-mentioned bearer quality of shares has been created for rational business operations and not for secrecy purposes.

Planned Activities in Hungary

1. Medical University and Clinics
2. Bio Engineering University
3. Various Agricultural Activities
4. Various Pharmaceutical Manufacturing Activities
5. Engineering Company for Domestic and Foreign Projects

The statutes of the Trust request that the assets of the Trust can be used only for humanitarian projects. The trustee decides about the nature of such humanistic projects.

The beneficiaries of the Trust have numbered accounts and their names are in a confidential file not available to the public. Under the statutes, the beneficiaries may receive only an amount per year equal to the providing of a decent and secure life for such an individual as he or she would receive based upon the average income a person with such a position might earn within the confines of his home country. In other words, in each country the standard of living will be considered to determine the amount payable to any individual in who is a beneficiary of the Trust, and that amount will be transferred into the numbered account of that person so that he or she may use that amount optionally.

The ratio between the asset and the paid-out benefits is about one to ten to the exponent nine. This means that the paid benefits are insignificant with respect to the assets of the Trust.

The Trust operates on an international level, however the business is always Related to the companies held by the Trust. The companies around the world function as profit-producing entities. The entire profits are paid back into the Trust and the Trust uses those funds for humanistic projects such as the afore-mentioned medical university and clinics.

This composition is very unique on an international level as it does not publicize a public company character. It does have profit-producing activities such as those listed below:

A. Building power plants in different parts of the world utilizing various forms of combustion including coal and nuclear. Depending upon the type of power plant, the investment requirements have different dimensions. A nuclear power plant, including its distribution network, requires invested capital approximating five-million US dollars and takes five years from inception to completion.
B. Various agricultural activities and projects
C. Erecting pharmaceutical manufacturing facilities
D. Various industrial manufacturing facilities for food products
E. Mining operations (Gold, Platinum, Diamonds)
F. Any other newly-established business

It must be understood that the humanitarian projects financed from the above profit-producing businesses income, do not provide for any profit to be withdrawn by any shareholders, as there are no shareholders. The benefits for the beneficiaries are insignificant, therefore, the entire organization can be compared from a financial point of view like a major manufacturing factory, where the workers, who produce the new products are the productive employees, and the administrative, or research, staff are the non-productive work force. What is meant by that is that they are non-productive in the sense of financial aspects. The increase of the capital and profit depends upon the sound ratio between the productive and non-productive financial ratio. The productive employees are the source of income, directly. The administrative and research staff indirectly contribute to the profit.

Taking all this into account, the above medical university and clinics, and the bio engineering university, are to be considered as non-productive activities; however, in long range, they also produce new discoveries, valuable patents, along with know-how and diversified economic values.

It, therefore, follows that the compensation for the employees can be much greater than the existing universities can provide.

In view of the above broader explanation, it can be realized that Godollo, Hungary, will become the international center for the Trust operation. The charts, which are a part of this report, will provide an overview about the entire system. The tele-medicine, which is to be performed through international television transmission channels, entirely and privately owned by the Trust, will become the connection among the small clinics and international businesses.

The technical operations in Europe will be centralized in Switzerland. The Computer International Network Center will be place din China. All data is continuously to be fed into the central server system in China, however Florida and Godollo, Hungary can have access to all necessary data.

By the latest technology (IBM / ITT) conferences, business and scientific meetings can be organized utilizing tele-communications. Therefore, the foreign chief officers do not need to travel to the headquarters. The conferences can be held before a big screen, projector in the local Hungarian, Chinese, or American facility. This kind of system requires a very substantial capital investment, however the Trust has enough financial strength to construct the most updated technical center.

It must be remembered that Informatic has a crucial role to gather information both in the scientific realm and the business territory. In Godollo's planned special institute, linked to Florida, they will be employing Hungarian expertise, whose German and English language knowledge qualifies them for that very essential position.

All employees will have five-year renewable contracts with very attractive yearly salaries and fringe benefits. The fringe benefits are health insurance for the employee and family members living in the same household, paid vacations, and additional bonuses from the international profit-producing business income, based on certain chart directed percentages.

Since the business produced profit will be reverted to the Hungarian enterprise, the source of necessary capital will always be available, without impacting the U.S. and Chinese capital requirements.

Other Issues

It is to be understood that the Trust Charter requires a file on the scientific background showing the various expertise of all potential employees. The necessity for this procedure is obvious since every major institute or university evaluates the credentials of proposed candidates for different positions. The candidates during certain periods of time will have accumulated scientific articles by various known writers who are accepted into the scientific community, as well as those who have submitted materials to highly reputable journals, periodicals, and other printed materials.

The evaluation process will be based upon the quality, and not the number, of articles. Under quality, it will be understood, in certain fields published within the same subject, that such articles will be compared to existing works with the final outcome that the article under evaluation shall reach the highest level of international acceptance.

The Trust, after receiving such articles, will send the material to various, independent scientific institutions, which have expertise in the subject matter under evaluation. The Trust will use absolutely independent institutions to avoid any conflict of interest so that the evaluation process will not be related to any special financial interest.

In order to obtain an objective evaluation, the Trust shall always choose an institute of non-conflicting interest. To elucidate the notion of the objective evaluation, one can understand that any scientific article written by a scientist, that is financially directly or indirectly supported by, for example, pharmaceutical companies, must be scored according to reduced factors when completing the evaluation, so as to not be influenced by such financial interest. They must also contain well-structured diagrams.

It is obvious that the clinical trials must be financed by some sources. If the financial support is provided by a pharmaceutical company, there is a balancing power required in the competition, whereby the article is always under the magnifying glass of the competitor pharmaceutical company. It is known that many controversial subjects emerge continuously. The controversies, however, after a certain period of time, are dissolved by the newly discovered scientific facts.

In most of these fields today, the accepted standards after a certain period of time become obsolete and need to be replaced by new proposals. Thus, the characteristics of the clinical trials bear the time-obsolescence factor.

Insofar as the subject of the filing and evaluation procedure, it can be understood that an invitation to perform a lecture, proposed by a pharmaceutical company for a physician, is not to be considered as scientific fact. It demonstrates, rather, the credentials of the invited physician. Otherwise, the pharmaceutical company would not approach the pin-pointed doctor.

The already received materials and the list of literature attached to the *'curriculum vitae'* are to be the subject of the evaluation process.

The final decision is to be in the hands of the chairman because the received scores are only recommendations.

The international aspects are the main frame of the system and it shall be organized even before the construction work will be completed."

Dr. Sandor Mihaly

CHAPTER THREE

Silent Trust Development Program (SDP)

THE FOLLOWING IS A report on the Trust activities including the World Bank Club on how the moving of currency is operated and controlled by the Bank Club on world affairs. What is included there is so powerful and, perhaps, unbelievable that, for the first time, ordinary citizens can see for themselves how the world is controlled, and by whom all major financial decisions are made.

Most citizens think that their government leaders make their own decisions on world affairs. I am afraid not, as money talks and money holders make these decisions.

Also, most citizens believe that their leaders or royal parties only think of their citizens. Again, I am afraid not, as they think of their own protection first. The Swiss Trust handles all that for them, assuring them of its safety in the Trust's possession, as it operates the Silent Trust.

Dr. Mihlay wrote a report as Chairman of the Swiss Silent Trust to explain its operation. When he completed this confidential report, he specifically wanted it NOT to be exposed to anyone. However, after his passing, his wife commanded me to let the details of the Trust come to light, as she was his power of attorney in this matter.

Before I open the book on the Silent World Government, I had an agent of the Trust approach me as he was in bewilderment over the Trust's progress, and whether any of the Doctor's programs would ever start. In response, I wrote the following verse:

There was an honorable gentleman who:

Listened weekly and received weekitis

Prayed weekly and received kneeitis

Which in time, he received arthritis.

His cure was to receive funditis

Which, in turn, developed startitis

Which, in turn, developed workitis

Listened weekly and received weekitis

And longed for retiritis.

But, fate has it that his funditis

May be coming due next week and

He will develop travelitis

In addition to Startitis,

And workitis.

The definition of '...*itis*' is a suffix in words denoting an inflammation or disease affecting a given part of the body. Therefore, in summary, we both have mentalities.

Regarditis,
Martin Olson

THE SILENT TRUST

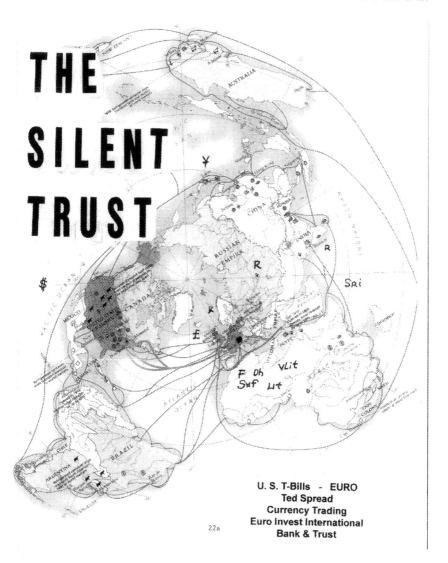

U. S. T-Bills - EURO
Ted Spread
Currency Trading
Euro Invest International
Bank & Trust

22a

Confidential and Proprietary Internal Memo

CONFIDENTIAL!

Internal Memo
Only for Internal Use!!!

YOU ARE ALLOWED TO READ THIS MEMO BUT YOU ARE PROHIBITED FROM COPYING IT OR LEAVING ANY COPY OF IT IN THE HANDS OF OTHERS, EXCEPT THAT YOU MAY GIVE A COPY TO THE AUTHORIZED GENERAL COUNSEL OF EUBT.

THE INFORMATION IN THIS MEMO IS HIGHLY CONFIDENTIAL. ANY DISCLOSURE OF THE INFORMATION IN THIS MEMO WOULD CAUSE UNPREDICTABLE CONSEQUENCES; THEREFORE YOU ARE INSTRUCTED TO CAREFULLY SECURE THIS MEMO IN YOUR MOST CONFIDENTIAL PERSONAL FILES.

----

(1) *Silent World Government*

(1a) It is not widely known that there is a so called *Silent World Government* behind the concept of the *New World Order.*

(1b) This *Silent World Government (SWG)* is made up of persons or institutions that have not been elected: the most powerful persons and financial groups, who held their first secret meeting in Bilderberg (Europe) about two decades ago.

(1c) The *SWG* convened their most recent meeting *during the middle of 1995,* in Switzerland, in *Bürgerstock* lies beside the lake, near Luzern. There is an historical castle there.

(1d) In this castle there convened, in a most secret meeting, several heads of state, top bankers, top officers of multinational USA, German, Swiss, British companies, the chairmen of major banks, and a few selected journalists, who committed not to report about the existence of the meeting, nor any names of participants.

(1e) The top members of the *Bilderberg Group* (hereinafter *BG* are well known personalities like Rockefeller, Kissinger, former President Bush, former President Reagan, President Clinton, the chairmen of large Swiss and German banks, Helmut Kohl (President of Germany), Mrs. Thatcher (former Prime Minister of Great Britain), many silent members of political parties—and representatives of large "trusts," among them one Swiss attorney, based on my instructions.

Confidential and Proprietary Internal Memo

(1f) The meeting in *Bürgerstock* was silently prepared by the Swiss Government, with no press advertising. It should be noted that *the castle of Bürgerstock is owned by the Trust*, under my jurisdiction.

(1g) Only the local journal in Luzern reported in a short article; that an international *business meeting* took place in the castle with the consent of the Swiss government. The entire area within a ten mile radius was sealed by the Swiss Police. Top participants, like Helmut Kohl and representatives of the royal families of Belgium, England and Monaco, arrived during the night *by Helicopter*.

(1h) No journalists were allowed in the meeting. Peter Jennings/ **ABC**, who is member of **BG**, and a woman from the **Washington Post**, were the only journalists present, since *they committed not to report anything* about the meeting and the subjects.

(1i) Since its organization, the **BG** has always had secret meetings *every six months* in Switzerland; the subjects are the global economic and political situation and what kind of actions must be taken to *push the official governments* to act on an international level.

(1j) Sometime prior to the G7 meetings, the **BG** decides what shall be on the Agenda of the next G7 meeting and *what decisions* shall be made.

(1k) It should be understood that the Iraq War was decided by the **BG**—former Presidents Bush and Reagan are members—and based on decision of the **BG**, Bush got started to work out the international coalition.

(2) Nothing Occurs in the World Without Decision of the BG

(2a) The signatory below, (Dr. Sandor Mihaly) controller of the Trust, has the full listing of the secret members of the **BG**, and all programs which will be presented to the next secret plenary meeting(s).

(2b) *The SWG holds the financial power in the entire world.* The world has been divided into three areas—[1](The US, Central and South America), [2](Europe, the Middle East and Asia), and [3](African Continent).

(3) *BG Operates through World Banks Club*

(3a) The **BG** or **SWG** are only popular expressions, referring actually to members of the **World Banks Club** (hereinafter **Banks Club**), which holds the power in the entire world. This tremendous power is represented in the United States by powerful families like the Rockefellers and the DuPonts, and in Europe by the Rothchilds and the Vatican, the Prince of Monaco, the

Confidential and Proprietary Internal Memo

Prince of Liechtenstein, the King of Belgium, and by kings and other celebrities; they control the worlds largest banks.

(3b) The basic decisions are in the hands of the **Banks Club**, who are a transparent group, that is they never appear before the public. The Chairmen of the major Banks are employed by the members of the **Banks Club** and they are subordinated to that world power.

(3c) This club is headed by the owners of the world's largest banks and not by the bank officers (who are only servants)!

(3d) Politicians are also only servants, because they personally have no control over the big assets, and *they therefore depend on the SWG* for their power.

(4) *The Banks Club Controls World Organizations*

(4a) The international organizations, like the United Nations (UN), the International Monetary Fund (IMF), World Bank (WB), the General Agreement on Tariffs and Trade (GATT), and many others, are indirectly under control of the **Banks Club.**

(5) *Banks Club Controls the World Economy*

(5a) From after the end of World War II, during the past approximately thirty five years, the **Banks Club** has operated on an international level, and its members have jointly worked out a method which makes it possible for them to control the world financial conditions, the world economy, politics, *and also, indirectly, governments.*

(5b) From above—*only from above*—it can be understood that the economy of the entire world is controlled by the so called **Banks Club**.

(5c) The domination of the world by financial tools can be described only by insiders who are part of the **Banks Club**. Outsiders have no knowledge about that mechanics.

(6) *Mechanics of the Banks Club's Financial Power*

(6a) Following is a brief explanation of how the **Banks Club** achieves such financial power.

(6b) There are, in all the world, only about 2500 members of a *currency trading association* that is operated by the Banks Club. Together, the *members of this trading association have a very substantial credit worth.*

Confidential and Proprietary Internal Memo

(6c) The banks use the monies deposited by their customers, during the period after business hours, until the next morning when banks open their doors for their customers.

(6d) The Banks pay interest on the money deposited by the customers, about 4-6 percent in USA dollars, calculated per annum, depending on the length of the deposit.

(6e) However, during the off business hours, the same Banks use the customers' monies for trade in the vast *international currency exchange markets.* In Europe, in only one day, twenty-four hours, the trading volume on this market is *USD 1.2 Trillion* equivalent hard currencies, *and 80% of this total is traded in Switzerland.*

(6f) In this currency trading, which is computerized, the Banks obtain a profit of about 50-80% per annum. This means that after the Banks pay to their deposit customers an average of only 5% per annum, the Bank retain the big difference for themselves as Bank earnings.

(6g) From these huge profits, the Banks then buy government

securities such as US treasury bonds, or G7 government bonds, thus becoming **LENDERS TO THE GOVERNMENTS**.

(6h) The Banks also use these government securities as collateral to borrow funds from the central banks, and *they then invest these borrowed funds back into the international currency exchange market operations.*

(6i) The *end result* is that *the government of the USA is world debtor,* like other governments, and the **Banks Club** is the *lender.*

(6j) Thus, one does not need to be a genius to conclude how the **Banks Club** dominates the governments of the world and how the **SWG** exercises its silent, transparent power worldwide.

(7) *The EUBT "Self Liquidating System*

(7a) Before proceeding further, it is necessary to review Chart No. 1: the *EUBT Self Liquidating System.*

(7b) If the EUBT Self Liquidating System is to be understood, it must be analyzed from the point of view of the *interest of the Banks Club.*

(7c) EUBT uses the system of the **Banks Club** (the Trust is a member of the **Banks Club**), with the essential difference, that EUBT's profit from the international currency exchange will be given away to the country, and will not accumulate and increase the asset of EUBT and the Trust, (indirectly the **Banks Club**'s asset).
Confidential and Proprietary Internal Memo

(7d) The **Banks Club** holds, through brokerage companies, about 80% of the assets of the world, in the form of loans and securities—the remaining 20% is in form of deposits from Bank depositors.

(8) *EUBT's Self Liquidating System Contrasted With Banks Club's Sinking Funds System*

(8a) *The Sinking Funds System is controlled by the **Banks Club**, but the EUBT Self Liquidating System is not under power and control of the **Banks Club**.*

(8b) The **Banks Club** *Sinking Funds System* requests that the substantial part of a specified capital shall be deposited with a major bank (a member of **Banks Club**), obtaining the low interest for the depositor, while the Bank uses the same monies to achieve large multiples of profit of which the Banks must pay out to the depositors only a little fraction. (See Paragraph 6.)

(8c) If the *Sinking Fund* has been structured for a term of ten years, due to the inflation factor (6% per annum), the portion of the earned interest that is returned to the depositor will be offset by the inflation— therefore it will not work.

(8d) *The EUBT System is not the Sinking Funds process. The EUBT Self Liquidating System uses the* **Banks Club** mechanics, but the profit from this system *will be converted into industrial facilities.* And since EUBT has 70% of the shares of the industrial companies, EUBT obtains the profit from the industrial companies, or to state more accurately, returns the profit from the industrial companies to the owner of the EUBT, that is, to the Trust.

(8e) However, there is *a big problem, an obstacle or administrative challenge,* that must be eliminated. EUBT is a private bank and therefore has no cash service facilities for transactions. Therefore, EUBT uses companies owned by the Trust as vehicles to transfer, or to handle funds *by major commercial banks*—(members of the **Banks Club**).

(8f) Under the **Banks Club** *Sinking Fund System,* profits go to the members of the **Banks Club**, but under the **EUBT** *Self Liquidating System,* substantial funds *are diverted for the benefit of the participating country.*

(8g) Therefore, the **EUBT** *Self Liquidating System* is counter or contrary to the interests of the **Banks Club** members. the **EUBT** system can be said to represent **A THREAT** to the interests of **Banks Club** members if it becomes a **PRECEDENT!**

(8h) Therefore, **EUBT** would be entirely isolated from the international financial community, and the companies of the Trust, which are the essential vehicle to perform this silent development program, would find *no banks to cooperate with them,* for obvious reasons.

(8i) Therefore, to overcome this major obstacle, **EUBT** has worked out the so called *Reverse System.*

Confidential and Proprietary Internal Memo

(9) *The EUBT Reverse System and Silent Development Program*

(9a) Before considering an outline of the **EUBT** *Reverse System*, the Chart No. 2: *Ownership Family Trust* must be understood.

(9b) The **EUBT** *Self Liquidating System*, (which is not connected with the **Banks Club**), provides major developmental assistance free of charge to participating countries, through foreign investment, to generate very substantial industrialization programs, without using the modern colonialistic method as the **Banks Club** members do. (See Paragraph 6 again).

(9c) Therefore the **EUBT** *Self Liquidating System* takes away the huge profits that would otherwise go to the **Banks Club** members and donates those profits to the participating country.

(9d) The logical questions are, then, (9d-1) if profits under the **EUBT** system are donated to the participating country, what is the financial interest of the Trust (**EUBT**), and (9d-2) how can the *Self Liquidating System* be hidden from the knowledge of **Banks Club** members, since **EUBT** must use the top prime banks as *pass through* depositories of funds? (Since *cash* does not appear as a physical note, or as *legal tender* the public uses to purchase little items—the cash inside the banking system exists only as a book entry, in our out—therefore without difficulty, it could be verified in the books of **Banks Club** members that the **EUBT** *Self Liquidating System* indirectly takes away profit from the **Banks Club** members, and if this *Self Liquidating System* would be known in the open market, world financial interests would recognize that the controlling power of the **Banks Club** is threatened.

(9e) By the combination two major elements, the inhibiting factor that is described above can be eliminated entirely, ***and*** the interest of the **Bank's Club** is threatened only TEMPORARILY, because after bank aspects of the transaction have been completed, the *diverted funds* in the form of Bank letters of credit will be redirected to the members of the **Banks Club**—multinational companies, the manufacturers of equipment, goods, etc., use the same **Banks Club** members.

(9f) Now the reader may review Chart 2: *Ownership Family Trust* (See Separate document, No. 378—Chart 2: *Ownership Family Trust*).

(10) *EUBT Silent Development Program*

(10a) As a part of understanding Chart 2: *Ownership Family Trust*, it is well to review Chart 3: *Silent Development Program* (See separate document, Chart 3: *Silent Development Program*).

(10b) This latter chart contains the so called *Reverse System* whereby (10b-1) the funds, as Chart 1 shows, are provided by the Trust, and (10b-2) the money offer becomes only a tool to hide the *Self Liquidating System;* but of course the funds would never need to actually be drawn.

Confidential and Proprietary Internal Memo

(10c) The KTT, which is a standard bank technical tool, provides a customary proof that the funds are available in the form of a one year loan, again, by standby letters of credit issued by the first top twenty-five prime banks (all members of the **Banks Club**).

(10d) Therefore, the acting banks will see nothing less than the same system to which they are accustomed, whereby they wait for the funds, with the usual expectations, (again, Paragraph 5 describes the mechanics of the **Banks Club**'s processing and squeezing system.

(10e) If we consider the daily USD 1.2 Trillion trading volume, the USD 300 Million in every fifteen days reflects only USD 2 Million per day average, a sum which will *not even be noticeable to Banks Club members.*

(10f) As the end result of this protocol, LUSD 60 Million will be diverted from the **Banks Club** in every fifteen days, and these funds can be processed without any time limitations, because the system is set up so that the same funds of USD 300 Million will be used repeatedly by other customers to the **"Banks Club**, namely T.Co(1), T.Co(2), T.Co(3) ... T.Co(-).

(10g) As Chart 2 shows, the system provides that of the shares (100 total shares), 30% are provided free of charge to the partner (private)—since it will be self liquidated, and the trust retains only 70% instead of the full 100%--however the 70% will provide for long range industrial profit.

(10h) The industrial development projects established in the participating country will assure jobs, and the local population, that is, the workers, will have decent incomes and be assured of financial security for their families, for the long range—and therefore the population will support the policy of the government.

(10i) In every fifteen days, the USD 1 Million cash, that is allocated for the 30% shareholders, provides good incentives at the front before the dividends would start to flow to the numbered accounts in the *Trust*.

(11) *Summary*

(11a) For the government central bank, the risk is zero.

(11b) The participating country will receive the benefit of substantial development programs, without investment.

(11c) The Trust receives, in every fifteen days, USD 1 Million. This incentive money is part of the ***EUBT*** *Self Liquidating System*, and therefore, is not taken out from any project related investment funds, and consequently it is not a bribe.

Confidential and Proprietary Internal Memo

(11d) The 30% of shares will be transferred to the same Family Trust, without any charge, because also part of the "Self Liquidating System."

(11e) The dividends will be expatriated to the Family Trust (30% of the shares relating dividend).

(11f) For each project, another new company shall be established; the 30% shares are connected with many companies, not only one of them.

(12) *Procedure*

(12a) At the start, EUBT, the Trust, and T.Co(1), shall make an application or short presentation to the proper government agency. This presentation shall be made by T.Co(1), and in the same time, the government Bank shall assign an account to T.Co(1).

(12b) It is to be understood, that EUBT and the Trust must remain transparent, only the T.Co(1) operates in front.

(12c) The proper government agency shall issue a permit to T.Co(1) to operate in the country through a newly established domestic company D.Co(1), that shall then be established, and be ready, when the first cycle of USD 300 Million is processed. (Shares [70 + 30]% -- all foreign shareholders).

(12d) The documentation for "Protection against Nationalization," and the "Dividend Export Permit" shall be issued to T.Co(1) – which is the owner of D.Co(1) and exercises the control from abroad.

(12e) Any documentation, regarding the single project shall be subject to operating meeting, however the process, what the SDP will realize, in general terms shall be recorded in a memorandum which is integral part of the documents, (as Par. 3).

(12f) The KTT shall be provided immediately, and in the interim time all paper work will be completed within few days.

(13) *Conclusion*

(13a) The One Million incentive will be available in about eight banking days after the KTT is received.

(13b) Temporarily, the USD 1 Million that is to be dispensed in every fifteen days, will be handled by **EUBT** until the Family Trust is completed.

END

/s/Dr. Sandor Mihaly

Martin Olson

Memo from Martin Olson to Dr. Mihaly as an update to financial activities:

23 Sept,1994
Dr
Memo;   Additional report.
1. Book, Global Dreams 1994 about global economy stated that following facts.
   1. 5 out of 6 dollars are electronic transferred.
   2. 2 trillion USD per day move by electronic network.
   3. Cost of transfer is ¢,18 cents.
   4. Money a truly global product. Eurocurrency accounts all over the world
      1987 was 4 trillion.
   5. Bank of International Settlement is 640 billion a day.
   6. Currency trading never closes. 30% of Asia market, 45% doing trading in
      Europe and 15% in US trading facilities.
   7. Average trader currency wage is 65,000 year.
   8. CitiCorp earns 150 million, currency trading every quarter.
   9. 1980 to 1985 volume of international loans fell from 100 billion year
      to 25 billion. New notes/bonds gradrupled 50 billion to 200 billion.
      Eurodallar lending market went from 25% in 1980 to 85% in 1986.
   10. Every day estimated 150 billion in US Government bonds change hands
      across global trading network. In US 1992 US owed 2.7 trillion in
      Treasury obligations to private·investors. 17% are outside of USA & 1
      trillion held by Fed Agencies.
   11. Today scrubbing dirty money is easier. Electronic transfers are SECRET.
      Grand Cayman has highest concentration of fax machines in the world.
      To serve its 548 banking outposts which hold assets of about 400 billion
      "I can hide money in the twinkling of an eye from all the bloodhounds
      that could be put on the case" William Mulholland, Chief excutive office
      of Bank of Montreal. 50% of money traffic resides in or passes through
      a tax haven.
   12. "CHIPS" privately owned by 11 NY Banks, service available to 142 particip
      banks globally. More than 150,000 international tranactions a day. CHIPS
      moves 2 billion a minute and is the largest in the world which interact
      with SWIFT (1000 banks), Bankwire (200 US banks) & CHAPS-British
      contribution to settlement of international accounts. WE have had direct
      talks with the President of CHIPS, John Lee as well as with SWIFT.

2. REport on RSA from US State dept in detail. including their 5 year
   reconstruction & developement program (10.5 billion) including building
   one million new homes. 40% unemployment expected to grow to 50% rest of
   decade. Report dated July, 1994. Outlook is next few years is postive with
   an economic boom. Provided economic conditions globally is up.
   Report approx : 30 pages.
3. Cigna Insurance called. They operate in 51 countries. They own their own
   Insurance company in China and Indonesia and operate a large insurance
   company in South Africa. They stated that they will call me Monday on ther
   ability and whether they can be more competetive and save money on coverage
   I am dealing direct with no broker or agent.
   I am dealing direct with the director of Global Risk Management of Cigna.
   Allan May.

Regards
Martin

CHAPTER FOUR

Trust Self-Liquidating Funding System

THE FOLLOWING REPORTS AND explanatory charts on the Trust, and its visions and goals for a medical university and clinics, as well as a bioengineering university, were made by the Doctor.

Again, these reports by the Doctor reflect his ideas and goals, and give the reader some insight into the Doctor's thinking.

For example, the accompanying memo of agreement written in 1993 between the Trust's Bank, EUBT, and the Peoples Republic of China, demonstrates the size of one of the Doctor's projects. The provisions of this agreement would be that the EUBT would provide to China 50 billion U.S. dollars as a start-up investment, which would eventually escalate to 500 billion U.S. dollars, for the integrated economic development for the whole of China, through EUBT's self-liquidating funding system with no budgetary cost to China.

Currently, China is hamstrung by its 50 billion U.S. dollar world bank debt.

The Trust's self-liquidating funding system is actually funded by their off-hour currency trading system in Switzerland.

This memo of agreement, prepared by the Trust through EUBT, was forwarded to Hong Kong as shown, without being signed, and depicts the size of the projects in which the Trust became involved. Whether the agreement was actually signed and funded was only known by the Doctor, as members of his staff were told things only on a need to know basis.

EXPLANATION OF CHART 1

SELF LIQUIDATING SYSTEM

The Trust, controlled by Dr. Milhaly has liquid assets of about USD one hundred billion, in the form of G7 securities and stocks of banks and real estate, net value of approximately fifty billion USD – in different G7 countries, under titles of complex trust system, which are protected by the local governments against law suits by "asset protection laws".

The Trust is the owner of private merchant bank, which has no involvement nor connection with the public. The total assets of the Trust belongs to families, accumulated through several generations, during a period of about 150 years. The Beneficiaries are represented by numbered accounts which receive, pursuant to the original Trust provisions, each year only so much money as will assure the families of successors a decent life style.

The statute of the Trust gives general guidance that the assets of the Trust can be invested only and exclusively in humanistic projects at a minimal financial risk.

In the event of incapacity of the Trustee, who shall be only one person, qualified and having a diversified education, and if the Trustee shall have no successor(s) from the owners family, qualified, the Trustee shall be replaced by experienced bank officers, who shall be selected by an arbitrary method, This means that the Board of Trustees must be composed by five persons whose names and identities shall be selected by statistical probability methods – like the winner of the "lotto" are selected. By this system the continuation of the operation of the Trust has been assured into the distant future.

#

Chart 1 – describes how the system works.

Explanation of Chart 1

From the assets of the Trust a package of government securities (example, US Treasuries) will be sold to a major Swiss bank for cash (1).

EuroInvest International Bank & Trust Ltd. (EUBT), which is owned by the Trust, receives 300 million USD cash (2).

The 300 million USD cash is divided (3) into two sums, 240 million and 60 million. From this division (4) 60 million is transferred to a company, owned by the Trust. This company is the "front operator" concerning the SDP (Silent Development Program – Chart No. 2). This company uses commercial banks (members of the "Banks Club"). **HOWEVER**, only 60 million goes to the commercial banks.

The other portion of the funds, 240 million, will be used for trading foreign currencies in the currency exchange market (see Paragraph 6 of the introductory "Confidential" Document). EUBT uses, conservatively, only a 50% projected profit margin in estimating profits from the currency exchange market.

In one year 240 million produces 120 million profit, non-taxable (Liechtenstein – tax free). As (7) shows, from the 120 million profit, 60 million is the "Self Liquidating" part and will be used for projects (5). The other 60 million is added to the original capital, 240 million, and the 300 million asset returns to the Trust.

#

The above, of course, is only a very short conceptual representation. In practice the operation runs by a sophisticated computerized system and the trading is very fast. In actuality in one hour one trader executed about 20-30 trades.

It should also be understood, that the 60 million profit in the real world can be obtained only after a one year operation.

The Chart does not show that the 60 million will be "internally" borrowed from the Trust, against "internal collateral" which means by book entry, since the funds never leave the controlled system of the Trust.

(4) shows that every fifteen (15) days begins a new tranche of 300 million (1), with the same mechanics. The "years end" for the 60 million tranches will be for each consecutive 300 million tranche shifter by 15 days.

The assets of the Trust are sufficient to allow the procedure to be repeated every 15 days. Therefore, in 300 days, which is the "banking year", there is already 1.2 million USD free of charge for direct investments.

Chart 1 does not show that the invested available funds, after industrial production starts, provide new profit as a dividend, and that said funds will be fed back into the recycling system.

#

It shall be emphasized that in the case of a loan to a government against a central bank guarantee, each portion of the produced profit of 120 million, as shown on the chart, cannot be produced from the borrowed fund, in contrast of the EUBT system. The loan shall be amortized by the borrower, therefore, the yearly amortization capital part, plus interest, during a period of a 10 year loan, requires double or even triple repayment of the principal borrowed sum. This serves as a convincing argument that the "sinking fund system" to repay borrowed funds is an incorrect concept, used in the banking business by unexperienced people.

The "Banks Cartel" dominates the world, therefore, the EUBT system **MUST BE USED SILENTLY** and this is why it is named the "Silent Development Program".

#

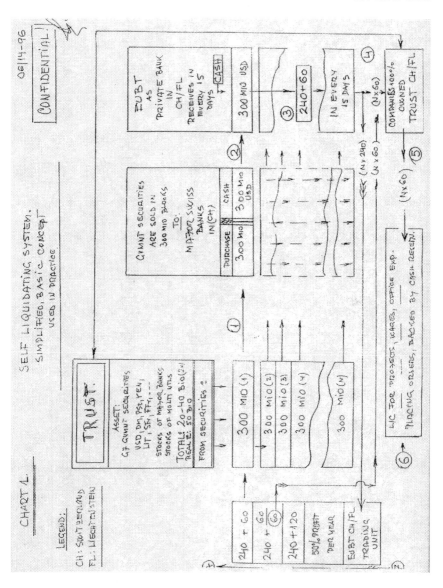

EXPLANATION OF CHART 2

<u>FAMILY TRUST</u>
"Ownership"

The law in Liechtenstein (Europe) protects the assets of a family by a very special entity, translated into English, "Family Trust" (in German language: "Stiftung"). (5) A Family Trust is a legally independent entity.

The beneficiary (or beneficiaries) of the Family Trust controls the numbered account at major Swiss Banks, protected by the bank secrecy laws. Therefore the identity of the person cannot be disclosed by the bank and cannot be discovered by any third party.

In the country where the SDP works, for each project there shall be established a domestic company, D.Co(1) with two major foreign shareholders. P.Co(1) is a speical offshore company which owns 30% of the shares of D.Do(1). The remaining 70% of the shares are owned by another offshore company, T.Co(1) which belongs to the Trust (which provides its assets for the implementation of the SDP).

As (2) and (5) show, P.Co(1) is owned by the Family Trust. The Family Trust receives the dividends from D.Co(1) –30% - and also the one million dollars which is received every 15 days. Both sums will automatically be deposited to a numbered account at a major Swiss bank in Switzerland.

This numbered account is 100 % controlled by the "Person" (1), who is the signatory of the account and decides what to do with the money.

Mostly the signatory of the numbered account rests a safety deposit box from the same bank and all documents, credit cards, etc. are in that box. Therefore, when the "Person" arrives in Switzerland has access to the contents of the box, including the money.

There are many legal aspects concerning the successors of the Person, however, in the statute of the Trust there is always listed the future beneficiary, successors, and all legal subjects that shall be considered during the construction of the statue of the Family Trust. There is legal advice available from EUBT and the Chart shows only the basic concept of the Trust operation.

For each project there shall also be another domestic company to which will also belong a different P.Company – therefore d.Co(1), P.Co(1) and D.Co(2),P.Co(2) and so forth. However, only one Trust is needed.

We have to refer again to the "Banks Club" operation. The profit, composed by the 30% dividends and the one million cash received every 15 days, indirectly has been provided by the currency exchange operation, previously explained, which is part of the "Self Liquidating System". The "Banks Club" members never would give away this profit and the profit of the Trust. They would rather lend the money to the country against the guarantee of their central bank, if the bank is strong enough. The strength of the central bank is represented by the countries economic position, trade balance, inflation, etc. parameters. By lending to the country the Banks Club protects its profit position.

In the case of the SDP, the personal benefit and benefit for the country by the EUBT system, is indirectly a very heavy and damaging competitor for the members of the "Banks Club", therefore the "Reverse System", referred to earlier, must be used.

Martin Olson

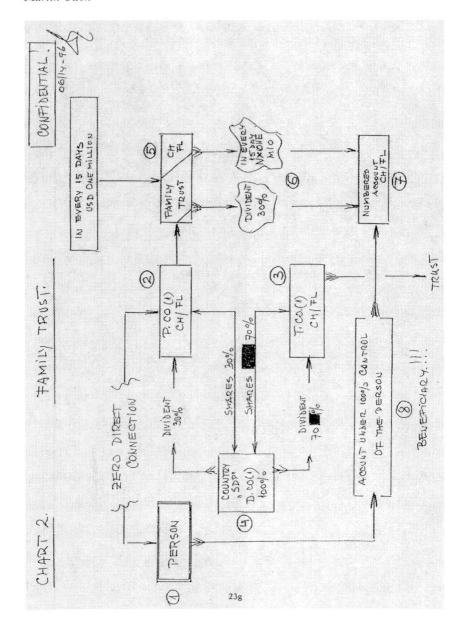

48

EXPLANATION OF CHART 3

SILENT DEVELOPMENT PROGRAM
BANKING STRUCTURE

This part is the most simple one from a banking mechanics point of view, however, behind this banking process are global, world wide existing relations, concerning the power of the "Banks Club".

IT CANNOT BE EMPHASIZED STRONGLY ENOUGH THAT THE SELF LIQUIDATING FINANCIAL SYSTEM **MUST BE KEPT CONFIDENTIAL ON THE HIGHEST LEVEL**, BECAUSE ITS FIRST STAGE IS AGAINST THE VITAL INTEREST OF THE "BANKS CLUB".

The world is entirely controlled by the Secret World Government (SWG), through the Banks Club. EUBT, by the Trust, is connected with the SWG, (reminder to the ownership of the castle in Burgerstock, Switzerland), therefore with different philosophical background the same mechanics that the Banks Club uses, can be utilized for the benefit of the developing countries and in the second phase, whereby the orders will be placed in form of Letters of Credit the members of the Banks Club will be satisfied and they will not see any threat.

The first phase must be perfectly isolated from any oversight possibility from the side of the major commercial banks, i.e. from the members of the Banks Club.

Chart 3 shows, again in simplified form, how the EUBT financial recycling system can be made transparent from the observation of the Banks Club members.

It must be understood first of all that the Trust used so called "front companies" whose function is to set up a "conventional banking process" only "pro forma"! "Pro forma" means in this case that the commercial banks (3) see nothing other than a usual conventional financial arrangement and process and therefore pay no attention to it.

The front company of the Trust, with the Trust in the background, are indirectly connected with several other companies (4) owned also by the Trust (T.Co(1), T.Co(2), T.Co(3),...T.Co(n)having accounts with the commercial banks (3)

The function of the front company (2) is to make transparent the other companies (4) which are the acting companies, as investors, and source of funds, for the Silent Development Programs. In this way the front company ISOLATES the "T.Co(n)" companies (4) from the "sight" of the commercial banks (3). Consequently, "T.Co(n)" companies can act freely without any disturbances by the Banks Club.

For each single project there shall be established a separate company in the country of the implementation of the "SDP", (5), known as "D.Co(n)" companies. (Remark: for memory-technical purposes in the charts, the companies, owned by the Trust are named T.Co(n), and the Domestic companies are named D.Co(n), etc.)

Domestic companies establish in the countries of the SDP are perfectly transparent concerning their activities to the commercial banks (3), therefore any leakage concerning the self liquidating system is perfectly sealed with respect to the banks (3), the members of the Banks Club. These companies do not have accounts of (3) related banks. They have account only in the SDP country with the bank owned by the government of the SDP country. T companies (4)/(6) also have accounts with the same government bank.

Chart 2 ("Family Trust") shows the relationship between T and D companies, which has previously been explained. A short review of Chart 2 at this point would be helpful.

> D companies are owned by two "foreign" companies, P and T, whereby P companies are Personal companies [P.Co(1)] are not disclosed to the government as to how they are linked to the family Trust.

> Chart 3 ("SDP") under (1) contains a remark that all documents shall be kept in Switzerland/Liechtenstein to protect the anonymity of the "Family Trust" structure.

D companies shall obtain from the government certain documents and permits (7). These documents will be presented to the banks (3), (2) by the majority owner T to demonstrate that they are doing legitimate business in the country of the SDP, <u>without any reference to the SCP</u>.

The critical question NOW can be understood, as to how it is possible to implement the "Self Liquidating System" without any knowledge of the Banks (3), members of the Banks Club.

The members of the Banks Club will be shown the "Reverse System". Under the Reverse System we need to understand that the country DOES NOT NEED TO LOAN MONEY FROM THE BANKS (3), BECAUSE <u>THEY HAVE THE NECESSARY FUNDS</u>!

How can we show that the country does not need money, that it only needs foreign companies who are in the position to deliver technology, industrial facilities and all kinds of programs which are in the development plan of the government or of the country on a <u>turnkey basis</u>?

P and T companies, as West European companies have this ability and have already been accepted by the government because they have recognized the necessity of the establishment of D companies and have issued, or promised to issue documents (see Chart 3, (7).

Here we need to understand that all funds derived from the complex operation, as Chart 1 (Self Liquidating System) shows, together with the Self Liquidating System MUST BE KEPT HIDDEN.

The transparency of the Self Liquidating System will be performed by the "Reverse System". However, in the real world the funds which ARE AVAILABLE from the Government Bank never will be needed, because the funds are available from the Self Liquidating System. "Reverse" means that we, the government, have the funds, we do not need to borrow it, we do need only executors of the programs!

The above goal can be reached without expenses and without any risk from the side of the government bank. Nothing else shall be executed other that the Key Tested Telex to a major European Bank for the account of the FRONT COMPANY of the Trust which KTT shall be allowed to expire. This process shall be repeated every 15 days, always using the same test of the KTT and sent to another reference company T.Co(1), T.Co(2), T.Co(3),...T.Co(n). See Chart 3 (8) and (9).

For the Banks Club (8) will appear. However, (9) (expiration of the KTT) will not appear (11) because the funds will be provided by the Self Liquidating System and Banks as shown on Chart 3. (3) cannot see that by the KTT indicated funds have been provided and replaced by EUBT funds through T companies having accounts with banks (Chart 3 (3).

The text of the KTT is attached hereto as Exhibit X or Exhibit Y, as the situation may require, together with an explanation of the KTT.

Chart 4 "Silent Processing" shows that the USD 300 million is not needed from the government band because the Trust provides collateral for the SBLC. This collateral passes to EUBT and the resulting SBLC is issued by one of the 25 to 30 top banks in Europe (members of the Banks Club). From the front company the SBLO will be exchanged by the Trust for cash, this cash asses to T.Co(1) and from there to the "Self Liquidating Process".

The remark was made concerning Chart 1 which demonstrates the Self Liquidating System, that it is "simplified". Now that remark can be understood.

It must also be understood that the Trust/EUBT is related to the Banks Club. However, the Trust is transparent for the banks of the Banks Club because of EUBT as a bank has the same position as the other members of the Banks Club.

The described system is <u>UNBREAKABLE!</u> due to bank secrecy laws and the fact that no information is available and no law requires the information to be disclosed to the public.

#

The central and government bank is not exposed to any risk or disclosure. The KTT has only the purpose to enter in the circle of the Banks Club and make possible to use the Self Liquidating System "through" the member banks of the Banks Club, without any possibility of interference by them.

On the second phase, whereby T.Co(1) places orders from the accumulated USD 60 million, the Banks Club will have the usual benefit because the multinational companies will have very substantial accounts with them and during the progress of the industrialization, they will make a profit from the orders and related business derived from the Self Liquidating System.

THIS PAPER IS HIGHLY CONFIDENTIAL AND CANNOT BE COPIED AND IS ONLY TO BE READ BY TOP LEVEL PERSONS. ANY DISCLOSURE WILL HAVE IMMEDIATE CONSEQUENCES, BEING THE WITHDRAWAL OF THE TRUST AND EUBT.

NO FURTHER INFORMATION IS AVAILABLE.

ANY CONVENTIONAL CHECKING, REQUEST FOR REFERENCES OR CREDENTIALS IS NOT AVAILABLE. THIS IS NOT AN OFFER!!! THIS IS ONLY AN EXPLANATION, WITH HISTORICAL FACTS. EITHER IT WILL BE UNDERSTOOD AND ACCEPTED OR NOT.

BASIC PRINCIPLE "TAKE IT OR LEAVE IT".

DR. SANDOR MIHALY
CHAIRMAN

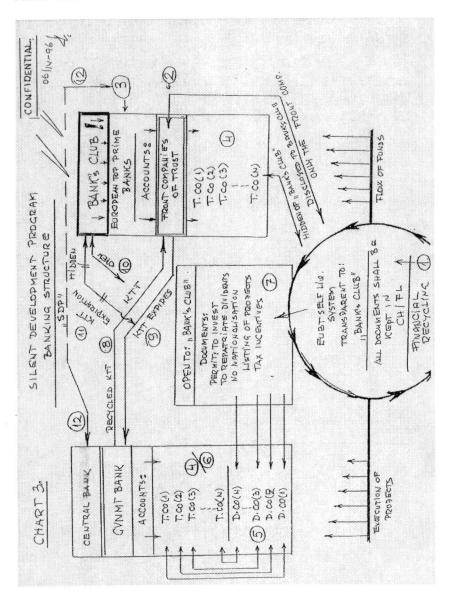

EXPLANATION OF CHART "RCY"

THE COMPLETE BANK PROCEDURE

––––––––––––––––

This Chart is essence is a composite of the entire system with certain elements not included in order to allow comprehension of the chief points more easily.

The Chart shows only one single cycle whereby in usual operation the cycle will be repeated every 15 days.

"X" shown the crucial essence! The capital for investment is generated by the activation of the asset of the Trust (C) and therefore a draw of funds from the government bank (B) IS NOT NEEDED.

The reason for the necessity of the KTT (2) has been previously explained. However, the question may arise, "Why is it not possible to invest the capital directly, without the use of bank (B)?

It shall be understood that the investment capital is composed of 60 million tranches (6) whereby each tranche of 60 million is a "free" portion of the whole investment capital which does not need to be repaid to anyone because it represents PROFIT. This is why it is possible to give away 30% of the ownership of the shares "free of charge" as shown on Chart 2 (Family Trust)..

The production and generation of the tranches of 60 million shall be made invisible for the members of the Banks Club, since the interest of the Banks Club is to obtain the 240 million tranches in the form of a deposit where the deposit would be used like (F) does. Consequently (F) does not deposit the 240 million with the members of the Banks Club, instead it operates in the currency exchange market to obtain profit for itself. This possibility exists only for (F) because it is a private bank, 100% owned by the Trust. However, the shares of (F) are bearer shares and therefore it is not possible to verify the "Owner" (Trust).

(F) operates on the currency exchange market with the participation of the members of the Banks Club because (F) itself is a member of the

Banks Club and among themselves occurs the global trading of various currencies.

(F) is not a public bank and its function as a bank is limited because it does not take deposits from the public. It uses only the assets (funds) of the Trust (its owner) (C), and therefore its membership regarding the Banks Club is limited only to the currency trading.

If we assume that (B) is not incorporated in the processing system and the KTT (2) is not being used, then it is not possible to provide for the Country a USD investment in the amount of 15 billion because the assets of the Trust (C) should be used as collateral to borrow funds from the Banks Club (in the theoretical case (F) would not exist) for which loan be received about 10% interest per annum and amortize the loan during the life of the loan. By this loan situation the projects (manufacturing plants) would have very heavy financial burdens. The substantial portion of the yearly profit of the industrial units would and should be used for such payments. At the same time the members of the Banks Club would obtain 60-80% profit per annum for themselves in currency trading.

At Barclays Bank (Bahamas) appears (B) Bank like a prospective lender, whereby against Standby Letters of Credit offers funds to the Bahamas Company. This formal situation reflects a customary bank/borrower relationship, therefore no one sees and exceptional case.

The text of the KTT (2) has been formulated in such a way that BA(Co) Ltd, cannot take down funds even with the SBLC because (B) is in the position to deny to wire funds. Namely the KTT does not specify the banking details and by the time that specification would be settled the KTT would have expired. Barclays Bank (G) does not "See" that the capital is not provided by (B). Barclays sees, that after KTT (2) has been received, the capital funds through (E) bank channel have been received and therefore the KTT has no more significance and thereafter expires, which is normal.

The importance of the Central Bank (A) has significance during the verification process which is carried out by (D) on behalf of BA.Co.Ltd. The verification process is important for the simple reason that it is a means whereby (D) can verify that the KTT (2) indicated sum at (B) is available. (It will NOT be taken down!)

From the above it follows that the amount indicated in the KTT does not need to be deposited at (B) because (A), as the controlling entity, covers the phase of "availability" and that means that (B) can provide in accordance with the terms and conditions in the KTT, which not yet set bank to bank basis and NEVER WILL BE!

The above verification process triggers the entire process as Chart 1 (Self Liquidating Process) shows.

No legal problems exist since from the banking regulations point of view because in the KTT indicated conditions shall be specified. Without specifying the conditions funds cannot be drawn, therefore this position is safe for both (A) and (B).

From the "Domestic" point of view the system is also perfectly in order because at the same time as Chart 3 indicates, D.Co.Ltd applies for various permits concerning the projects. (Note: P.Co.Ltd. is 30% owner and T.Co.Ltd has 70% ownership in D.Co.Ltd., as Chart 2, Family Trust, indicates).

Chart "RCY" shown that the funds by (H) are "free capital" however Standby Letters of Credit go tot he members of the Banks Club. The system does not give away (5) funds (240 Million) to the Banks Club, but one part goes to the Banks Club (10).

Chart 1 (Self Liquidating System) indicated that the 60 million (N x 60 million) will be available only at the end of one year currency exchange market operation. However, all financial steps are under the full control of the Trust (C), (F) and (H), and therefore without any financial risk the Trust (C) can provide from its asset enough to "lend to themselves" "in advance" each 60 million, whereby this fact appears at (4) in the form of 360 million, from which the 60 million (12) through (H) and (7) will be used to place orders (10). This financial transaction part in the books of the Trust will be shown as an in-out between columns and therefore properly accounted for.

From the whole system follows that after verification has been completed (3A) nothing happens other than "wait" until the KTT (2) expires. Through (B) is not exposed to any risk. NO FUNDS TRANSFER (3B) because the funds as "X" shows, by the actions of (C) goes in the system.

(6) shows that 60 Million goes to (H) and 240 million is routed along (5) to (F). The use of 240 million by (F) can be seen from Chart 1 and Chart 4.

On Chart RCY the circle represents pro forma the "recycling" process as above indicated on Chart 1 and Chart 4.

##########

The entire system is composed by many very precise, simple steps which in turn are based on very simple logic. When coordinated properly the result is "X" FUNDS FROM TRUST AND NOT FROM GOVERNMENT BANK. This makes possible 15 billion USD "free of charge" investments, based on 70% - 30% joint ownership plus a bonus of one million USD every15 days.

END

THE CHART "RCY" AND THIS EXPLANATION ARE PROPRIETARY AND HIGHLY CONFIDENTIAL. NEITHER MAY BE COPIED NOR SHOWN TO ANYONE ELSE WITHOUT SPECIFIC WRITTEN PERMISSION.

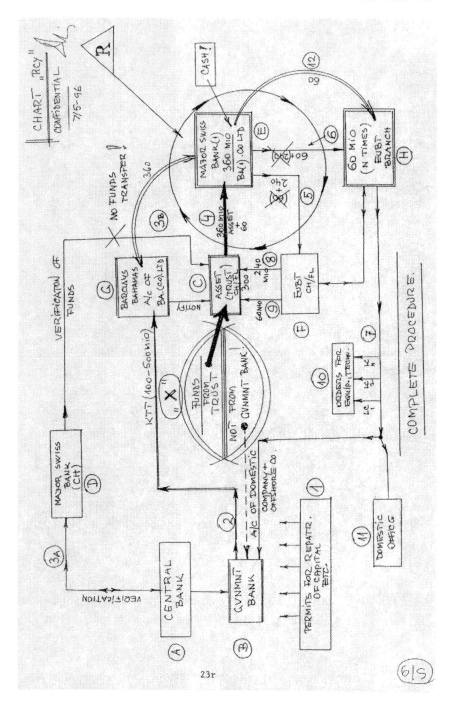

THE SWISS SILENT TRUST
EXPLANATION OF THE CORPORATE STRUCTURE CHART

The Office of the Director of the Swiss Secret Trust will be in Godollo, Hungary.

The advisory staff shall consist of persons with expertise in various subjects, as determined by the Director. Their function shall be to advise the Director in selected areas, based upon the tasks required of the chairperson for each section. The advisory staff members will have no decision power. They will function solely to present their reports to the Director in writing.

The Director will summarize the received reports and present them to the chairpersons in writing for approval. If any additional items shall be added to the proposed materials, the chairpersons will provide to the Director a proper explanation, as well as directives, as to what and how such materials shall be modified.

The communication between the Director and the chairpersons shall always be confidential. No one will have access to any information about the contents of such communications.

Under the domestic activities listed are different categories, which are subject to oversight, as well as those domestic activities related to international involvement. For example, any engineering or construction related use of budgetary funds has the possibility of being abused by the lowest level working employee, therefore, controlling of spending is a task to be supervised by an oversight director.

In the case of foreign subjects, only that which is linked to domestic activities is to be supervised by the oversight director. Any foreign spending is to be supervised directly by the chairperson's office in charge of that project.

Medical facilities will be supervised only in the domestic area.

Export/import activities are related to various fields since equipment, machinery, and spare parts either will be imported or, after completion, will be shipped abroad to various facilities.

Informatic related spending shall be supervised in the domestic area, however the domestic staff of Informatic has always maintain a connection or interrelation to foreign entities.

All details will be working out during personnel sessions between the Director and the chairpersons concerning proposals.

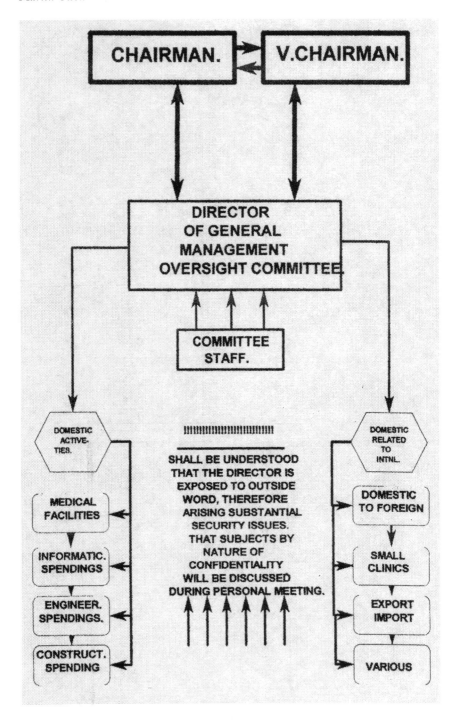

GENERAL MEMORANDUM OF AGREEMENT

Transaction Code: EUBT-MH/ST-SINO-DPPC/933-HK

Reference Code No.: 378-CHI-001

KNOW ALL MEN BY THESE PRESENTS

THIS GENERAL MEMORANDUM OF AGREEMENT is executed and entered into by and between:

EUROINVEST INTERNATIONAL BANK & TRUST (EUBT), a private Investment Bank and Trust, licensed and operating under the laws of West Indies, United States of America and Switzerland and engaged actively in WORLDWIDE banking activities through its offshore investments and operations, with mailing address at P.O. Box 15288, West Palm Be ach, Florida 33416-5288 United States of America, represented in this Act by Lucio E. Himbing, Jr. in his capacity as ATTORNEY-AT-LAW REPRESENTATIVE AND APPOINTED BANK TRUSTEE OF EUBT and as per fax Instruction from the Bank Chairman/President/CEO dated 26 February, 1993 under Reference Code No. 378-CHI-001, and hereinafter referred to as FIRST PARTY

AND

The Government of the Peoples' Republic of China, represented in this Act by Honourable, the Chairman of the Bank of China (BOC), Hong Kong and hereinafter referred to as the SECOND PARTY

WITNESSETH

1. WHEREAS, EUBT is a private investment bank and trust endowed with Missionary Vision and in-depth commitment to help and assist THIRD WORLD DEVELOPING COUNTRIES and its people achieve true freedom through economic emancipation and national development and people empowerment.

2. WHEREAS, EUBT has a unique TECHNO-MICRO ECONOMIC SYSTEM which could provide fund without commercial bank funding syndication, in the amount of about FIFTY (50) BILLION UNITED STATES

DOLLARS roll over sequences up to US$500 Billion within a longer period of more than 10 years for INTEGRATED ECONOMIC DEVELOPMENT for the whole of China, whereby the "EUBT SELF-LIQUIDATING Funding System" DO NOT REQUEST ANY BUDGETARY COST from the Government of the Peoples' Republic of China.

3. WHEREAS, EUBT in addition to the legitimate Funding resources that EUBT can provide without cost to the Government, NO interest, NO repayment, EUBT has in its NETWORK worldwide the most modern technology and manpower expertise to undertake the optimum development and utilisation of P.R. of China's vast economic agricultural and industrial potentials in the field of PETROLEUM GAS AND OIL, AGRICULTURE, TRANSPORTATION, STEEL manufacturing and modernise its COMMUNICATION SYSTEM and transfer of technology to the mainstream of China Manpower Resource.

4. WHEREAS, the P.R. OF CHINA despite of its huge and very rich natural resources and positive climate of investments such as political stability and peace and order, it cannot accelerate its nationwide dispersal Economic programmes because it is hamstrung by its US$50l-Billion World Bank debt and do not have the necessary Funds to boldly implement all the Government long range programmed Economic and Industrial projects that shall usher solid and sustaining Economic prosperity and political stability to the Country.

5. WHEREAS, it is guaranteed that by availing the EUBT self-liquidating TECHNO-MICRO ECONOMIC SYSTEM, P.R. of China shall surely be catapulted to its rightful throne as a self-sustaining economic and political leader in World Power, particularly in Asia-Pacific nations.

NOW THEREFORE, based on the foregoing premises, the First Party (EUBT) and the Second Party, representing the Interest of the PEOPLES' REPUBLIC OF CHINA, have mutually and bilaterally agreed to become PARTNERS in the Total Economic Development of the whole of China with the Noblest of Objectives and purposes and bilateral commitment, to WIT:

CLAUSE I

That both parties, EUBT and the GOVERNMENT OF THE PEOPLES' REPUBLIC OF CHINA shall jointly pursue and implement the projects already listed and programmed by the Government under its 10-years to 25-years Economic Development and Industrialisation plans and priorities.

CLAUSE II

That EUBT shall be responsible to provide all the necessary funds under its SELF-LIQUIDATING MECHANISM in about 50 Billion US Dollars to 500-Billion US Dollars through EUBT TECHNO-MICRO ECONOMIC SYSTEM with no cost to the Government of P.R.of China.

CLAUSE III

That, against the package funding by EUBT, the P.R. of China shall provide Promissory Bank Notes (PBN) to be issued by Bank of China and/or Bank of China Hong Kong confirmed by Bank of China, Beijing – said PBN to conform the Mechanism to be jointly approved by EUBT and P.R. of China and EUBT guaranty with full banking responsibility that the PBN shall only be deposited in the EUBT Bank Vault and protected by complete secrecy and confidentiality without recourse.

CLAUSE IV

That the Government of P.R. of China shall allow assist and authorise EUBT to implement the Government's aligned Economic and Industrial Projects such as construction of OIL, GAS, PETROLEUM, REFINERIES, STEEL PLANTS, INFRASTRUCTURE, MINING, ENERGY PROGRAMME, AGRICULTURE, COMMUNICATION SYSTEMS, setting up and operating all kinds of factories that are export and manpower oriented in the whole of China without cost to the Government.

CLAUSE V

That EUBT shall provide all the modern TECHNOLOGY AND

MANPOWER expertise, that guaranty the OPTIMIZATION of Economic and Industrial profits for the OVERALL benefit and progress of the Country and the Chinese people.

CLAUSE VI

That the Government and the states of the P.R. of China and the people shall become the EVENTUAL OWNERS of all the projects undertaken by EUBT under its self-liquidating TECHNO-MICRO ECONOMIC SYSTEM without interest and costs to pay.

CLAUSE VII

That EUBT guarantees that all its funds are of legitimate source being audited by the FEDERAL RESERVE Bank every 90-days, and that EUBT shall only endeavour to work for the maximum welfare of China and the Chinese people.

CLAUSE VIII

That upon acceptance and signing of this General Agreement, a detailed MECHANISM of the EUBT TECHNO-MICRO ECONOMIC SYSTEM and IMPLEMENTATION GUIDELINES shall be drawn at Florida, USA and submitted within thirty (30) days for approval, ratification and execution between EUBT and the P.R. of China Government for commencement of fund infusion thereafter in accordance with International Monetary System and the starting of projects.

CLAUSE IX

That both parties and all the parties involved in this transaction shall have the obligation to maintain the highest degree of confidentiality and secrecy and that under NO CIRCUMSTANCES disclose and reveal the features and mechanism of this special EUBT Funding System to the International private business and financial community to avoid the intervention of the International Monopoly System.

CLAUSE X

All subsequent Addendum(a) shall be an integral part of this General Agreement

IN WITNESS WHEREOF the parties hereto affix their signatures this _____ day of March, 1993, at Hong Kong.

EUROINVEST INTERNATIONAL BANK AND TRUST

by: Lucio E. Himbing, Jr.
ATTORNEY-AT-LAW
TRUSTEE AND REPRESENTATIVE

BANK OF CHINA, H.K.

by: _____
         CHAIRMAN OF THE BANK

APPROVED/CONFIRMED:

DR. SANDOR MIHATY
     (EUPT CHAIRMAN/PRESIDENT/CEO)

P.R. OF CHINA FINANCE MINISTER AND/OR STATE COUNCIL

WITNESSES

1.   SPENCER P.S. TO
2.   DAVID C. PUN
3.   PAUL K.S. CHAN
4.   AILEEN TANG
5.   NANCY G. BARTOLOME

The following pages are taken from <u>THE INVESTOR</u> magazine, published by Hume and Associates, and are found under the section:

THE SUPERINVESTOR FILES

The title of the article is:

<u>The TED Spread</u>

The TED Spread™

*One of the world's most powerful strategies
for profiting from changes in interest rates*

On Jan. 31, 1985, many investors -- both beginning and
more sophisticated -- found themselves in a bit of a
dilemma:

- The stock market had soared to record heights just a
  week before. Putting money in stocks, even special
  situations, at that time would have exposed it to the
  risk of a substantial market correction -- a risk far
  outweighing the potential reward at those price
  levels.

- Commodities, with only a few exceptions, were mired in
  a long downtrend. Would the trend continue? Was a
  reversal due? Was the reward for guessing right worth
  the risk of being wrong?

- Bonds, responding to declining interest rates, had
  risen in price even more than stocks.

- Money market funds, reflecting the dip in interest
  rates, were offering the lowest yield in more than a
  year. And, while longer-term Treasury securities and
  certificates of deposit were offering higher returns,
  it meant locking up funds and possibly missing later
  opportunities for lack of cash.

Thus, for investors with cash on their hands -- whether a
few hundred dollars or a few hundred thousand -- it seemed there was truly nothing worth buying.

Yet, you know, as certainly as we do, that the markets
did not grind to a halt. People were buying, and people

69

were selling. And, as is always the case, some people were losing money while others were making it.

What you probably don't know is that some people -- experienced traders who might be classed among the "SuperInvestors" of the world -- were making enormous profits.

In fact, it's possible that on Jan. 31, 1985, the very day so many typical investors were confused, many of these SuperInvestors made an investment play that produced a profit of 107 percent in only a month and a half -- an annualized return of more than 817 percent!

And they did it with a minimum of risk -- risk that they clearly defined from the very beginning.

YOU CAN DO IT, TOO!

What is this powerful investment play -- this secret of SuperInvestors? The answer is The TED Spread -- and it's no secret. In the following pages, you will learn exactly how you can make the same play yourself, even if you have only a small amount of money to invest.

First, though, look at the two newspaper clippings show- ◀1
ing the actual prices for a T-Bill futures contract and a
Eurodollar futures contract on both Jan. 31, 1985, and
March 19, 1985. These were the prices for initiating and
closing out the play described above -- the one that re- ◀2
turned a 107 percent profit in only 48 days. Then, take a
look at the calculations showing the actual dollar values
and how The TED Spread produced that annualized gain of
817 percent.

Throughout The SuperInvestor Files, key tables, calcula- ◀ KEY POINT
tions, charts and vital strategy points will be featured
on the left-hand pages to help you better understand the
securities and techniques discussed in the text. These
features will be numbered and flagged in the right-hand
margin, right beside the points they illustrate.

And don't worry if you don't understand everything in this first example. By the time you finish reading this File, you will be able to not only read the tables, com- prehend the charts and follow the calculations, but to implement the strategy with the same knowledge and understanding possessed by SuperInvestors who do it with millions of dollars. This knowledge -- and the confidence it inspires -- is extremely important.

Why? Because The T E D Spread -- which is actually an acronym used by SuperInvestors in place of the more formal name, The T-Bill/EuroDollar Spread -- can very quickly become a mainstay in your personal arsenal of investment strategies. Opportunities to implement it occur with considerable frequency -- and returns of 100 to 200 percent on each play are fairly common, making annualized gains truly spectacular! ◀3

Many readers of The Hume MoneyLetter scored one such spectacular gain when Dr. Morton Shulman -- a self-made investment millionaire who would qualify as a SuperInvestor by any definition -- recommended they buy a TED Spread. The price difference between T-Bill futures and Eurodollar futures at that time was 130 points.

Only 33 days later, the Spread had widened to 215 points and the fortunate readers who took Dr. Shulman's advice had more than tripled their money. Their actual return on an initial cash commitment of $1,000, after commissions, was 202.5 percent -- an annualized gain of 2,239.7 percent!

By trading in multiple futures contracts, Dr. Shulman himself made TED Spread profits in excess of $20,000 during this one trading period. You simply cannot afford to ignore that kind of potential if you are to join him among the ranks of today's SuperInvestors.

So, read on. Then, when the next day like Jan. 31, 1985, rolls around (and they do roll around fairly often), you'll be among the select few who know how to recognize the key signals and exactly what to do to reap the maximum profits from the favorable conditions.

NOTES/CHARTS

Jan. 31, 1985   March 19, 1985

These clippings from Barron's show actual prices, in circles, for T-Bill and Eurodollar futures on Jan. 31 and March 19, 1985. What happened to interest rates between those two dates could have given you a profit of $1,075 on a $1,000 investment -- an annualized return of 817 percent -- if you had known how to do The TED Spread! The following numbers show how:

January 31, 1985
   Buy T-Bill future   @ 91.79, or 9179 points
   Sell Eurodollars   @ 90.86, or 9086 points

      TED Spread   @ .93, or   93 points

Initial margin deposit: $1,000

March 19, 1985
   Sell T-Bill future   @ 90.61, or 9061 points
   Buy back Eurodollars @ 89.25, or 8925 points

      TED Spread   @ 1.36, or 136 points

  Gain on Eurodollars: 161 points x $25* = $4,025
- Loss on T-Bills: 118 points x $25* = -$2,950

= Profit on TED Spread: 43 points x $25* = $1,075

  Return on $1,000: $\frac{\$1,075}{\$1,000}$ = 107.5% in 48 days

Or 817 percent annualized return
*--We'll explain later why each point is worth $25.

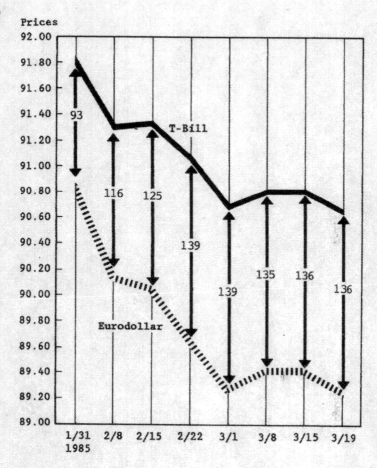

This chart shows how the spread between the price of T-Bill futures contracts (solid line) and Eurodollar futures contracts (broken line) widened between Jan. 31, 1985, and March 19, 1985. With a TED Spread, you do not need to be concerned about the direction that the individual prices move -- you are interested only in the actual difference between the prices, which in this case increased from 93 points to 136 points.

NOTES/CHARTS

4 *WHAT "MARGIN" IS*

When you "buy" a TED Spread, you do not actually spend any money. Instead, you put up what is known as a "margin deposit" on each Spread you buy. This margin deposit is really good-faith money that you leave in your account with the broker as your guarantee that you will live up to the terms specified in the futures contracts making up The TED Spread. The margin deposit initially required to do a TED Spread is not related to the actual price of the futures contracts involved, nor to their value in dollars -- it is set by the exchange where T-Bill and Eurodollar futures trade and is based on the volatility of prices (the more volatile the prices have been, the higher the margin requirement will generally be). Individual brokers can and do ask for higher margin deposits, but they can never require less than the minimum set by the exchange. As such, the required margin deposit for a single TED Spread may vary from as low as $250 to as high as $2,000. (The examples in this File use $1,000, which is a fairly standard margin requirement.)

If your TED Spread makes money, both your profit and your margin deposit will be returned to you when you "sell" the Spread. If your TED Spread loses money, your loss will be deducted from the margin deposit you put up and any remaining money will be returned to you. Should your loss grow too large (which should not happen if you follow the rules outlined later in this File), it may exceed the margin deposit you originally put up, in which case your broker may ask you to deposit additional cash. Your margin deposit is referred to as the "cost" of your investment in a TED Spread only because the money is tied up and cannot be used for other purposes. As such, it is also used as the "cost basis" for figuring your rate of return.

(NOTE: Do not confuse the margin deposit for an individual TED Spread with the minimum deposit a brokerage firm requires to open a futures trading account. That amount can be as low as $2,000, but will usually be at least $5,000 to $10,000 -- and can be even higher. A full discussion of finding a broker and opening a trading account will be included later in this File.)

OUTSTANDING FEATURES OF THE TED SPREAD

The TED Spread is a highly effective strategy for reaping
profits from the ever-changing level of interest rates.
It has been used over and over again by America's most
successful investors -- SuperInvestors who are constantly
on the lookout for strategies with the characteristics
offered by The TED Spread:

- The potential to earn 100 to 200 percent on your
  initial investment.
- The potential to earn from 300 to 500 percent if
  there is a major financial crisis.
- The potential for large profits whenever interest
  rates move up --- and the occasional possibility for
  profit even when they move down.
- A defined and limited level of risk that you can
  keep as low as $500 to $600, even after commissions.
- The need for an initial cash commitment (or margin
  deposit) of around $1,000 -- or less.

◀ KEY POINT

◀4

These characteristics make The TED Spread an almost perfect strategy for smaller investors with limited funds --
or for people who, though they may have more money, don't
want to take unnecessary risks. Yet, with only a few exceptions, this technique has remained part of the private
preserve of big-money SuperInvestors.

Why? The primary reason is that very few small or conser-
vative investors understand all of the ins and outs of
the strategy -- even though implementing it is really no
more difficult than buying and selling 100 shares of
stock.

It is so simple, in fact, that if you are familiar with
T-Bills, Eurodollars and futures trading, you could just
skip the next few pages and go on to Section II -- "How
To Do The TED Spread." The instructions there map out the
steps required to buy or sell a TED Spread -- and show
the best times to do it.

If you do skip Section I, however, you may not really understand how and why the strategy works. So, we recommend
that you at least read through this entire File, just to
make sure you have all the information you need about the

23hh

essential components of the trade. Together, Section I
and Section II will explain:

• The key elements of The TED Spread.

• How -- and why -- the strategy works.

• When and how to implement a TED Spread.

• Exactly how to place your TED Spread order with your
  broker. (If you don't have a broker, we'll tell you
  how to find one in Section III.)

• How to monitor your investment (which will take no
  more than five minutes of your time each market day).

• When and how to close out your TED Spread.

You will find the whole strategy no more difficult to follow than a recipe where all the ingredients are clearly
listed and each stage of preparation is described in proper order.

So let's start cooking up some profits!

CHAPTER FIVE

Projects and the Japanese Notes

THE DOCTOR HAD ME do studies on numerous projects such as petroleum refineries, petrochemical plants, shipping and finding crews to operate the bare boat charter tankers. I had to redo the studies many times to make sure that I covered all possible problems that could arise. This is the Swiss way of undertaking things, not the American way. I should have had his guidance in my younger years. I would not have made so many mistakes. The Doctor was very demanding but I was able to handle the work load. I was fascinated with the projects because I was learning something new every week.

In 1988, the Chairman, Dr. Mihaly, stopped all work for one year. Again, this was an instance of what I previously mentioned when I said that the doctor only released information on a need to know basis; and this was one of those time when I guess I just did not need to know.

So, my wife and I moved to New Hampshire to keep myself busy by becoming a representative for the Prudential Insurance Company. I could, at least, earn some money while I was on this hiatus.

At the age of 63, the Chairman asked me if I would come back to work on a very sensitive subject. I agreed and the following details were starting to unfold in small doses. I received a call from the Chairman the first week in 1989, explaining in some detail that the Trust controlled vast sums of Japanese government-backed bank certificates of deposit. What the Chairman wanted to do was to implement those CD's into a plan using U.S. Government guarantees for a program as insurance for third world projects, which in the end would result in taxes, and aid in the reduction of the U.S. trade deficit. He then sent an overview letter to me concerning the program, which outlined the following: The Trust files five-billion U.S. dollars equal in Japanese yen in 1986 with U.S. Customs in Washington, D.C. The Trust is working through Japanese Nationals, who are working directly with the Minister of Finance, Central Bank, to develop the transaction by using these securities so that they may not upset the International Money Market, and since these securities are private, there is no requirement to file with the Security Exchange Commission. An additional problem would be to operate with such a large amount of cash on the Currency Exchange International Market, which would trigger an undesirable shifting concerning the YEN/USD exchange rate provoking intervention by various central banks in order to keep the equilibrium under control. The Doctor was given a Japanese name, Thigeyuki Maruyama, and it was used in his mail to and from his Japanese correspondents.

The Trust has worked out a special arms-length type of transaction to avoid the open money market. The basis idea is an 'Arms Length Borrowing System' The Chairman ended his instructions to me with an explanation that, with the Japanese Securities, the Trust would deliver to the U.S. Treasury, in the form of a tax, approximately 30 billion U.S. dollars within three months. Now this is 1989 and I am only told of a huge sum of Japanese CD's held by the Trust that has already moved five billion dollars in 1986 to the U.S. Treasury. Knowing the Chairman for some time, I also knew that I did not have the whole story, and something bigger is behind this project.

At this point in time, I am trying to assemble some kind of reasoning behind the Chairman's request. I also had to decide whether this, too, is a waste of time, as I had many experiences over the years wherein a number of his projects were put on hold for reasons still not known to me. The Chairman wanted me to go to Washington and meet with government officials to discuss the Japanese Securities, which can be tricky and dangerous; it's like going into the lion's den/ Another thought was, "Why me, when the Doctor has lawyers available to do the task." Now that I know the Chairman better, and the caution he exercises in all his dealings, he probably asked me because I would not misuse the information for any personal gain, and that I would tell him honestly about any reaction from Washington. I could tell this was some kind of a test by the Chairman.

So, with the above information, and at the request of the Chairman, I called Chief of Staff, Governor John Sununu's office to obtain the name of the proper person to contact. I followed up the call with a copy of the Chairman's instructions to Governor Sununu. Then I called the U.S. Treasury Secretary Nicholas P. Brady's office, who referred me to a Don Chiodo, who referred me to Meg Lundsager, the Director of

International Affairs. I then sent an outline fax letter to Ms. Lundsager as well as copy of a letter from the Chairman to Secretary Brady, explaining in some detail what I knew about this subject, as told to me by the Chairman. I then sent a faxed letter to the Department of Commerce Secretary Designate Robert Mosbacher containing the same brief outline that I sent to Secretary Brady. I, finally, called the White House to make sure that they received the faxed letter, which the secretary to Governor Sununu had told me was sent to the State Department at 3:00 p.m. The next day, I called the State Department, Japanese Desk, and was told that they never received the letter. So, I called the White House again and they gave me the number to the Central Control Center between the White House and the State Department to check for myself. I made the call and the young lady who answered my call went through the documents with me that passed that day, and she could not find the letter. So much for tight security and communications in Washington.

I did all of the above by telephone, by letter, or by fax up to this point. I called again, on the first of April 1989, at the request of the Chairman to the State Department, Japanese Desk Officer William Breer, to make an appointment to see him on the 19th of April at 2:30 p.m. I drove from New Hampshire to Washington, D.C. and met with Bill Breer for about an hour and covered all the points that had previously been sent to Secretary Brady, the White House, and Secretary Mosbacher. I remained overnight at a Virginia motel so that I could stop by and try to see Secretary Brady or Meg Lundsager but I did not realize that stopping by the Treasury was as if I had asked to see the Pope and had to go through blood tests, x-rays, and a urine test. I was asked by Lundsager's secretary if I minded stopping by their office on G Street to discuss the subject with the officials there. So, I trotted over to G Street, ninth floor, as a lamb to the slaughter.

After I passed an armed guard behind a bullet-proof window, I met two men who were polite and started to ask my reason for meeting with Brady or Lundsager. So I explained in some detail about the Japanese CD's and, the next thing I knew, they were examining by briefcase. They put me up against a wall and began searching me for any concealed weapons. Then they started taking turns in asking questions, and intimidating me so that I would say something either about the securities and/or about the Chairman. I told them the truth of what I knew at that point, and after a while, I felt that they were setting me up to report to them on a regular basis about the Chairman and the securities. They even stated that I may be detained. Then the man who was evidently in charge came into the room and said, "Look here, we know that the Chairman will come through and deliver, so you should stay with the Chairman." I offered them to take my passport if they wanted it. They replied, "No. You will need it." I agreed to keep them informed on a regular basis. I felt it was to my benefit as well as the Chairman's.

After about three hours in their detention, they walked me to my car, which was parked in the garage below. I drove out of D.C. directly and returned to New Hampshire, not knowing about what may happen over the next few days. The next day, I went into the Prudential office, where I had been working, and they received a call from the Secret Service checking up on me. Great relationship with a company. Nothing was said, only raised everyone's curiosity. The Chairman called me the following day to ask me to arrange with the State Department Japanese Desk, Bill Breer, to accept a call from the Doctor's Japanese law firm in Tokyo. I agreed and placed the call to Bill who agreed, as he was being transferred to Tokyo in about two or three months. By him giving that information, I was sure that he had received a call from the Secret Service.

The Japanese call was made on the 24th of April, 1989, at ten p.m. Tokyo time, or ten a.m. D.C. time, to confirm my meetings and fax letters to the U.S. Treasury, White House, and Department of Commerce. I then checked with Bill Breer, who confirmed later that the call had been made. All this told me that something bigger than I had already thought was big, was occurring. Everything on a need to know basis. The Chairman then called and asked me to call Senator Bill Bradley's office and Senator Bob Dole's office to confirm to them the status of the securities with all the details. Senator Bradley was out, traveling, so I talked to his assistant, Paul Chase. I called Senator Bob Dole's office and arranged a meeting for May third, 1989, at four p.m. with his assistant Carolina Sealy at the Capitol Building, Room S235. After that call, Carolina was going to check with Treasury on the move to the securities, which occurred on April 27, 1989. The amount of the Japanese CD's, a total of 16 billion U.S. dollars equal in Yen. The Secret Service did call me on May 11, 1989, confirming that the 16 billion

Japanese securities did pass through Los Angeles U.S. Customs. All these trips to D.C. consisting of two trips and one overnight was at my expense without reimbursement. Another test by the Chairman.

My wife and I moved back to Florida in August of 1989 to start work with the Chairman, again; at this time he was in California. The Chairman was not planning to move back to Florida until the end of 1989. One of the reasons for moving back to Florida earlier than the Chairman was due to my wife coming down with cancer, and surgery was needed immediately. This started a long process of treatments and a long road down hill party due to the greed by the medical profession. When the Chairman returned from California, he then explained in some detail, not all, about the source of these securities and how they came under the control of the Trust and the Chairman. He then stressed the importance of developing a detailed program to handle major overseas projects and how to control them from United States soil.

The Chairman finally started to explain the real source of the Japanese Securities, its total value, and the involvement of the Japanese to conceal these instruments and their important value to the U.S. deficit problem. The CD's first started out as redemption bonds issued by the government, of which a small amount (some two percent) is still in circulation, and were later exchanged for CD's. These CD's, carrying an interest rate, cannot be cashed in or used as collateral except with the approval of the Minister of Finance. When Dai-Ichi Kangyo Bank redeemed the bonds and issued the CD's in place of the bonds, which totaled approximately 600 billion U.S. dollars equal Yen, was twice the value of the bank. The bank gave these Japanese CD's, which are really issued by the Japanese Government, to Japanese Nationals. These Nationals could not do a thing with these securities, so they embarked on a search for someone to take control of these securities. They turned to Switzerland and ended up with the Chairman of the Trust.

There was a second reason why the Nationals were looking to find someone to handle these CD's, and that was because it was too dangerous to have these instruments in their possession for fear of being killed. These certificates of deposit were issued by Dai-Ichi Kangyo Bank, but as aforementioned, they were really issued by the Ministry of Finance of Japan, as all banks in Japan are under the strict control of the government. They represent a 'pass-through' account at the Dai-Ichi Kangyo Bank, which accounts are ultimately the obligations of the

Government of Japan, rather than the bank. These certificates represent a secret fund of money, which was initially established by General Douglas MacArthur to rebuild Japan. These funds were initiated by the U.S. Government at the end of World War II to rebuilt Japan so as not to accept any funds from the allies at the end of the war. These funds also represent not only U.S. paid funds to the secret MacArthur Funds but also reparation funds confiscated by the United States during the occupation by SCAP, the Supreme Commander Allied Powers. The securities sat mounting in interest value, at the control of the Japanese Government after SCAP completed its work of the occupation. The history of the early days of Japan, and it ability to control, is explained in some detail in the following chapters. It is important to note that one has to know or review the history of the Japanese culture, and how it operates and maneuvers, as to how it controls and protects its assets, and to assure its long range planning.

After reviewing all the Doctor's reports and his 'white paper' written to explain the details of the securities as to its history and the plans for the repayment of these CD's so as to benefit both Japan and the United States, it is only right that the United States benefit from the ever-increasing interest on these instruments, which have existed since 1946. These CD's were an asset of the United States, in its truest sense, until they were ceded over to the Japanese officials by a Presidential Decree and consummated by the Vice-President of the United States at the time of giving back Okinawa to Japan with all the improvements completed on the island with U.S. funds. Since the time of cession, or transfer of securities to the Japanese officials by the Vice-President of the United States, these funds have been controlled and grossly abused, by high officials of the Government of Japan, a number of whom have corruptly utilized very large sums of money from the fund for their own personal benefit. The Chairman stated in his white paper that he had completed documentation, based on legal research, made by widely known international experts, concerning the origin of the referred financial instruments. By historical terms, veritable proof can be furnished that the financial instruments represent a long range investment by the U.S. taxpayer, as seen from the channels that were followed during this period. As of 1991, the value of these instruments is approximately 600 billion-plus in U.S. dollar equivalent Yen. The Japanese Government officials who bargained for the ceding of these funds from the United States to Japan, as well as the return of Okinawa, was then Prime Minister Kishi. As stated earlier, one has to review all the events that have happened in Japan by the Japanese culture, the U.S. Government officials, the U.S. legal system, and the banking business private sector of the United States and their selfish interests.

Explanatory Seminar from Dr. Mihaly Concerning Letters of Credit and Certificates of Deposit

In April of 1991, Dr. Mihaly had an opportunity to explain the workings of the Japanese Certificates of Deposit (CD's) with respect to the difference between those instruments and Letters of Credit (LC's).

The Letter of Credit system is one of the world's oldest financial instruments based upon centuries of experience, and invented by the British even before the United States was born. Domestically, LC's, being very primitive papers, are practically nothing more than written checks, only have different appearances.

In the international arena, the LC system expresses, perhaps, the most general and most sophisticated financial relationship between buyer and seller in more than 260 countries, which adopted the same system through their own legislation. This means that international conventions regulate this system. From time to time, in Paris, the International Chamber of Commerce (ICC) modifies the rules by applying new circumstances. The general world-wide acceptance of the LC system cannot be used securely without the existence of the International Monetary Fund (IMF) as a regulating organization. Therefore, every country participating in the use of the LC system must be a member of the IMF, which governs the internal economic conduct in relationship with all the other countries of the world including the actions of their central banks by posing restrictions in some cases and providing financial assistance when necessary.

With respect to Certificates of Deposit, these are not widely accepted as a financial instrument. In return for a cash deposit, the bank gives the depositor a piece of paper, CD, whereby the bank promises to pay back the deposited amount of money plus certain interest upon a predetermined time. The piece of paper has no value until the bank honors its obligation to pay out the funds to the depositor or creditor.

Government bonds are much more widely accepted financial

instruments because the bond is backed up by the full faith and credit of the issuing country.

The Japanese CD's in question are worthless pieces of paper by themselves. The payee of the CD's never deposited one single yen at the Japanese banks. Instead, in a fraudulent manner, managed by top level individuals in Japan, the government bonds, which were derived from the Ministry of Japan funds, have been converted into CD's, collateralizing the CD's inside the Ministry of Finance System in Japan by the use of the above-mentioned fraudulent origin of government bonds.

May international rules and conventions, which were legislated in Japan, have been violated:

Crime Number 1 – Conversion of Ministry funds to government bonds

Crime Number 2 – Conversion of bonds to CD's

Failure Number 1 – CD's are non-collectible as they do not legally exist in terms of the definition of a CD

Failure Number 2 – The wide range of conspiracy, which resulted due to the above, made it impossible for them to be utilized by any Japanese organization or individuals in order to make money on these CD's

It was only bay accident that one of the Swiss Trust's corporations became privy to what had transpired. The Complex Industries Holding Company (CIH) analyzed all of the political aspects involved in the above situation and discovered the corruptions, including the international conspiracy between former President Richard Nixon and the Japanese Prime Minister. Since the year 1983, thousands and thousand of meddle men throughout the world have tried to make money on these CD's without any success.

The only way these CD's could be utilized was to follow the rules of the Complex Industries Holding Company. First would be to acknowledge the danger of an international scandal, including the jeopardy of the whole Japanese well-built and efficient economy, which would be by pressing the politicians to accept the CIH procedure, whereby:

1. Approximately 600 billion dollars (the supposed value of the CD's) would represent the entirety of the budget for Japan for one year.

2. The CD's, now in the hands of private companies, would show that Japan was being held as hostage by those companies. Namely, Japan would have a 100 percent deficit from day to day, which would mean that the International Monetary Fund (IMF) would have to take drastic steps to balance the situation. That would entail the immediate devaluation of the yen by at least 50 percent, which would cause price increases inside of Japan to rise by 50 percent. The entire Japanese economy, as well as all of its society, would collapse with inconceivable social and political consequences. The brokers, who had tried to make money on these CD's, had no idea about such aspects.

3. The CIH, however, was in a position to deliver all the CD's back to the Ministry of Finance system, within a certain period of time, free of any charges. Therefore, the Japanese budget and economy would not get hurt.

4. The structure of the CIH assured that the U.S. Treasury would regain the original American investment, so the Japanese Ministry of Finance would have a substantial revenue income.

5. The CIH was not looking for any punishment to be imposed upon the persons involved in the above conspiracy. It is not an investigative authority, therefore, ilt does not function to determine the who, what and when of the crime that was committed on an international level. The CIH acts legitimately in providing a remedy for the treatment of political problems and makes possible, through its designed structure, the assurance that no one will get hurt, and that all parties involved will have their justifiable share from a legitimate profit. From a legal point of view, the CIH, in essence, during a longer period of time, abolishes the consequences of the committed crime, thereby causing an obsolescence of punishment.

To recapitulate:

a. From a political point of view, all the CD's would be delivered back to the Ministry of Finance of Japan, free of any charges.

b. The CD's could be canceled in the books of the MOF, without any cost.

c. Bonds, which backed the CD's, also could be canceled. The cancellation of bonds could occur even without their physical control. This could be executed because the bonds have been converted to CD's, consequently, the collateral for the CD's were in the books of the MOF as publicly, non-registered instruments, therefore, the cancellation does not require a public filing. And this cancellation could be executed, since the chief instruments, the CD's, would be delivered back to MOF by CIH without cost.

d. No political repercussion would be caused.

The only possible solution:

Having the CIH as applicant, issue LC's in yen with the beneficiaries to be major Japanese multinational companies. The LC's would be backed up by the assets of the Swiss Trust. The LC's are valid, real instruments, without any relationship to the CD's because the CD's, remember, are non-collectible, and therefore, are worthless. The CIH will validate the LC at the MOF in Japan, and the MOF will put its stamp on the LC. However, the collateral of the LC (Swiss Trust asset) will not be used. Instead, CD's will be physically delivered into another location, other than the MOF. This will be a secret location and will be handed over to an officer of the MOF who is knowledgeable about the history of the CD's.

Simultaneously, as the CIH is handing over the CD's free of charges, the MOF will pay the LC to the Japanese multinational company, in cash, in yen. Then yen comes from the budget of the Japanese Government.

The payment of the LC is not a freelance money transfer. The asset of the Trust must stay behind the LC, and the MOF will provide a loan until a certain period of time, under certain terms and conditions.

The CIH will place an order, simultaneously, with the payment, to manufacture and deliver certain merchandise. These goods will be sold by CIH on the international market, whereby CIH will receive a profit of about 20 percent. The original amount must be returned to the MOF, since it is a loan and is not a drain down from the Japanese budget.

To the LC's will be attached the requested documentation as to ICC 400. Upon repayment of the loan plus interest, the new tranche of CD's will be processed with new LC's exactly as above.

From this procedure it can be shown that the CD's are playing no role in this system. The CD's never will be redeemed by the issuing bank and the issuing bank will never be approached concerning these transactions; The retrieval of the CD's is a simple physical act, without any direct financial content or value.

A political deal:

The political deal means that the politicians understand that the CD's can be retrieved free of charge only if they make possible that the LC will get paid to the Japanese multinational company in yen inside Japan. However, the MOF needs some arrangement whereby they must have the legal structure showing that the paid LC related amount is a temporary government subsidy until the capital is returned to the MOF.

Since the LC's are backed by true assets of the Trust, nothing illegitimate happens and do not need the approval of the Diet or any legislative settlement. Also, the rollover system makes it possible that, at the end of an even longer period of time (at least ten years), that all the CD's will be delivered back free of charge.

The above description is only a general one. In order to provide some feelings as to how complex the entire system is on an international level, the following will explain several aspects, which are entirely a concrete part of the present LC system.

A loan from the MOF must be interest-bearing. The contract between a multinational company and the CIH must contain all the terms and conditions, which are the normal course of international trading (i.e. price, FOB, CIF, etc.) as well as whatsoever may be determined as pertinent, all shipping parameters, quality requirements, inspection by bonded surveyor or laboratory, foreign currency exchange relating the type of calculative methods, risks, time value of the money in different currencies, contract guarantees, insurance, all cost factors, loading, freight, unloading, distribution, related contracts in different countries (language and legislative), loss, damage, repair, maintenance, and so many other necessary factors, which cannot be enumerated here. It would take a book to describe everything. The fees would be handled by means of securities on the European market. A good analogy is to a television. It is not necessary to know and understand how the electronics works; all one needs to know is how to turn a TV on or off, and how to switch channels. The TV serves its goal: that of unilateral communications.

For a greater impression, there are simple tables which show the mathematical formulas that are an integral part of any departmental job in handling LC's. The tables showing these formulas are the basis for all LC's, CD's, bonds, or whatever nature the financial instrument or payment system happens to be, including the movement of money, the selling or buying of money, prices, exchange fluctuations and so on.

It is an interesting theoretical point of view when one realized the same formulas can be used to calculate the population growth (census), the effect of immigration, inventory turnover, or the rate of growth of bacteria in medical experiments in a laboratory. The same formulas are used for measurement of the radio-activity, with time, or nuclear reactors, light absorption, with thickness for filters (photography), length of solids, with temperature changes, the spread of chemical reactions, with temperature changes (the entire plastic industry uses these formulas), and so on.

LC's appear to be simple financial instruments, yet they are part of the most sophisticated workings that can be described only through highly scientific mathematics. Because of that, one operator never has the overall view of an entire system. Even one department can handle only one small portion of the problems that can be involved. That is why the international monetary system, the money market, centralized in the United States in Chicago, utilizes mathematicians, engineers, computer experts, and economists. The money brokers do not need to know or have any idea what is behind the profit that he or she is making, only that their investment is making a profit. However, the whole system is broken down into simple elements. Top management, however, must understand each element of the entire system.

Dr. Mihaly is well-credentialed to operate the Swiss secret Trust. He is a medical Doctor with numerous fields of expertise. He is a member of the American Mathematical Association, a chemical engineer in Europe with eight years of university studies in that field. He has three years of economic and banking studies and has 25 years of experience in the field of theoretical economy and financing inside of the banking life, which he inherited from his father.

There are many doctors who specialize in certain fields of medicine (dentists, surgeons, internists, urologists, dermatologists, osteopaths, oncologists, and so one). However, a pathologist mostly works out of a central laboratory by which he or she can determine from an examination of samples from a doctor, whether or not the results dictate surgery or other treatment. Likewise, in the pharmaceutical industry, the pathologist, due to his or her vast theoretical background, manages not only the basic research, but being also a chemical engineer manages the theory of the whole manufacturing process without the need to be present personally in the factory. As such, Dr. Mihaly managed and coordinated the work of at least 180 scientists, engineers, and other experts. This has resulted in new drugs and their related manufacturing process and resulting economics.

Banking and financial activity of Dr. Mihaly encompassed only about ten percent of his total activity.

Other interests:

At one time, Dr. Mihaly had me oversee another proposal. It was called the Irish Satellite, a communications medium that was to be the largest in the world. I met with the CEO from Hughes Aircraft who was looking for financing for one of their corporations and a project that it was involved in. Before the meeting was officially arranged, the vice-president of Hughes Communications had their security people do a thorough check of the Trust, and particularly, its Chairman. Once that was completed, the CEO faxed me, telling me that they wanted to go ahead with the meeting. They obviously discovered that the Chairman, and the Trust, were exactly who I said they were.

The Trust was all set to move, right down to the wire, and then everything suddenly stopped. The reason in this case was quite legitimate. The wife of the Chairman, Gabrielle, a research scientist herself, was extremely sharp. She was a marvelous lady with a great sense of humor and very smart. When she attended any meeting on any subject, she had all the facts; she knew everything that had to be known about whatever it was that was being discussed. Dr. Mihaly put her to good use whenever he had any new project by inviting her in to be a part of the program. The Irish Satellite was no different. When she got through with the CEO from Hughes Communications, a division of Hughes Tool, he did not know what hit him because he was not well-versed in his subject. Two days after the meeting, the CEO called me and I told him what went wrong – he simply did not have a handle on his topic.

There were numerous other projects that had started and stopped for one reason or another. So, it was not always comfortable spinning one's wheels and getting nowhere. I was a person who liked to start and then complete a project. It gave me a feeling of satisfaction. To have false starts, or to have to stop midway through a project, was not very enjoyable.

HUGHES COMMUNICATIONS SATELLITE SERVICES, INC.

POST OFFICE BOX 92424

WORLDWAY POSTAL CENTER

LOS ANGELES, CA 90009

TELECOPIER TRANSMISSION COVER SHEET

DATE: 5/14/90   TOTAL PAGES: 1

FROM TELECOPIER: 213-414-5545

IF THERE ARE ANY TRANSMISSION PROBLEMS, PLEASE CALL FAITH 213-414-6839

TO: MARTIN OLSON   FAX #: (407) 672 4-93

FROM: Larry Driscoll   PHONE: (213) 414-68 2

REMARKS/SPECIAL INSTRUCTIONS

RW MANAGING DIRECTORS

Tr. factor mentioned that ther were two Managing Directors of the
trust b* *pe that handled legal   administrative issues. Are their
onyr, luergen Olbermann and hairer   tan?

wanted:

JUERGEN OLBERMANN.
HEINER FEHRMANN

THESE ARE THE TWO
MANAGING DIRECTORS OF
THE TRUST THAT HANDLE
LEGAL ADMINISTRATIVE
ISSUES.

42a

Thankfully, this was not the way things always went. There were some situations where I had made accomplishments and those are what kept me going. I know the Doctor had some wonderful ideas and some exciting projects in mind, but because he had so many irons in the fire, it was hard to know when any of them would reach fruition. His greatest hope was the international hospital and clinic with its administrative headquarters in Florida. He even had me design the buildings, which were to be magnificent. He had the Trust's assets with which to work, it was just time that was closing in on him as it challenged his health.

CHAPTER SIX

Japanese History and the MacArthur Notes

THIS CHAPTER WILL GIVE the reader some insight as to the culture of the Japanese people as well as the beginning of the history of the secret MacArthur notes and the Doctor's letter on the notes along with a letter from the Trust's attorney in Japan.

The total face value of the MacArthur notes was 600 billion U.S. dollars in Yen. It is now 2010 and the value of those notes, with interest, could be well over one trillion U.S. dollars. Not one penny was paid back to the United States taxpayers who are the final losers in the game of global political greed.

A full explanation of these MacArthur Notes follows in the next segment of this chapter.

"All Eight Corners of the World Under One Roof"

In the beginning, the Japanese considered themselves to be the natural rulers of their world. In 660 AD, the Emperor Jimmu (Tribal Chief) decreed laws to govern his people. Jimmu promised, "To extend the line of the Imperial descendants and foster right mindedness." Jimmu's belief was that his capital would be extended to embrace all of the six cardinal points (of the compass) and the eight cords may be covered so as to form a roof. This was known as the policy of Hakko Ichiu, which meant all eight corners of the world under one Imperial roof, or rule of the world, only as Jimmu knew. (1) This was the first Declaration of "Policy," a term the Japanese borrowed from the British and came to revere. It meant a form of government and a social organization all in one: "A way of life."

Yasuhiro Nakasone, Prime Minister of Japan, said it another way, as he probed the road that Japan was to follow in her future relations with Asia and the world. "Japan," he said, "represented the leadership of Asian culture, which was moving with America, the heir to European culture, to bring together two great cultures that would thereafter dominate the world." (2)

Japan, in a century and a quarter, since Commodore Perry opened Tokyo Bay and forced the Japanese to deal with the outside world on western terms, has never lost sight of the fundamental aim of dominating its environment. The Japanese believe this is their destiny, just as they believe in the superiority of their civilization over all others. This, including the Chinese from which they borrowed modern technology. (3)

At the end of World War II in 1945, Japan was a mess. Once the Japanese acknowledged defeat, they made themselves single-minded to rebuilding their world within a dozen years with Japan dedicated to become the world's leading shipbuilder. Japan's economy became complete within a generation and became the third greatest industrial power of the world. None of this would have been possible without their deep-rooted traditions, and the organizational skills of the Japanese people.

Mitsui, the world's oldest large-scale business enterprise, started its dynasty five years before the Pilgrims landed in New England. Mitsui, started its first bank in 1683, a decade before the Bank of England was founded. The power of Mitsui reached full scale after the first world war.

Foreigners gained access to Japan by force, and remained there on their own terms. Its intent was to force Japan to become civilized, as westerners viewed it. This meant conforming to European and Western standards of government, commerce, law, and social behavior. The Japanese leaders understood the enormous task of westernizing their country culturally, politically, and economically. This was led by Japan's Minister of Foreign Affairs, Inove Kauru, in the early 1880's. Japan's leaders set forth only intending to satisfy the minimum standards. These standards were recommended by western arbiters, and treaties were revised so that Japan could impose protective tariffs. Many of these protective tariffs are still in effect to this very day.

In order to allow continuity and growth in private business, it was necessary to establish business enterprises that were solidly rooted in some basic industries. These companies had to be financially secure and versatile to generate satellite companies. They had to be so well-placed that they could survive any type of crisis or disaster. These centralized dictatorial establishments had to maintain themselves in the highest degree and be capable, at any time, to overcome the worst difficulties. It was on this basis that the "Zaibatsu," unique Japanese agglomerates, became the massive building blocks of Japanese capitalism. (4)

Japanese secret societies, all being very versatile, were established in every part of Japan. The strength of these secret societies reached out to Tibet, China and Mongolia. Japanese men of enormous wealth funded these secret societies. Their task was to gather information, and to smuggle, sabotage, and assassinate opponents, and recruit informants or political allies. This was not a group you would want to reckon with. They called themselves "Shishi," men of high purpose. The best organized group was "The Black Dragon Society," supported by the most influential Japanese industrialists. (5)

Mitsui's Bussau had offices in the United States, China, Manchuria, Korea, India, and Indonesia. In their New York office, Branch Manager Tajima Shigeki, located in the heart of the financial district, conducted tremendous business with the Third World, dealing with food, raw materials, soft goods and munitions. Mitsui secured ninety percent of the stock in the largest U.S. cotton purchasing firm. They made other opportune investments that assured reliable sources of commodities and technology. One known venture was Standard Aircraft Corporation, with an investment of two million U.S. dollars. This investment was made just prior to the first world war. Over the next three years they realized a fourteen million dollar profit. Aside from the enormous financial profit, Mitsui received invaluable experience in aircraft manufacturing, technology, and design. This knowledge enabled Mitsui to exert indirect control over Japan's aircraft industry.

The Great Earthquake of 1923 created an economic paralysis to Japan. More than one hundred thousand people were killed. Tokyo, at that time, was the third largest metropolis in the world. To rebuild Tokyo, the Japanese Government floated bonds in the United States and Great Britain. U.S. companies such as Western Electric, Westinghouse, General Electric, Libbey Owens, Dollar Steamship Lines, Standard Oil, Associated Oil and Alcoa acquired or increased their shares in Japanese companies. With these major investors, new capital as well as new technology was introduced to the Japanese. After a period of extensive infighting amongst the Japanese industrialists, the Zaibatsu Chiefs had the major share of the pie. (6)

"The way of Strategy," written in Japanese, is "Ni Ten Chi" This is taken from the "Book of Five Rings" written by MiYamoto Musashi in 1645 A.D. and translated by Victor Harris. Musashi was one of Japan's most renowned Samurai Warriors. The "Book of Five Rings" is used by many Japanese businessmen of today as a guide for business practices in running their sales campaigns like a military operation. It is considered Japan's answer to the Harvard MBA. This guide to strategy is a way of life in Japan and is reflected in this book as to their control of difficult situations. This "strategy" was used in Japan's occupation and recovery period after World War Two when Japan strategically worked through U.S. banks, U.S. legal services, and U.S. politicians to regain their control. Through the Japanese high politicians and nationalists, Japan was able to take back Okinawa and regain . securities that were part of the secret General MacArthur Fund. This fund was originally designed for the purpose of rebuilding Japan; and its accumulated interest and assets represented repayment to the United States of American for aid and reparation of the second world war.

Russia's KGB now gets involved in this process by sending a woman agent to Japan and Hong Kong in order to make some dramatic attempts to gain control of a few of the security instruments from Japanese nationalists who were not under the control of the Trust.

This instigates an FBI roundup of all persons who attempted to cash in these securities. The FBI roundup takes place in Las Vegas, London, and Dusseldorf. Then the Japanese Secret Service sends one of its agents to the United States and makes illegal attempts to secure these instruments.

This book explains the program of a European Trust. The Trust was given control of much of these securities from Japanese Nationalists who, for fear of their lives, could not handle the securities. The Trust began implementing a plan between 1989 and 1990 to put these securities to work for the benefit of the United States and Japan. This was to be organized on a global scale. Japan and the U.S.A. Governments, as well as select private businesses would profit from the movement of these securities. The Trust, of course, would receive a fair profit from this course of action.

The future benefits to both the U.S. and Japan are spelled out in detail. The Trust had to make sure that both parties would not lose and that they fully understood the consequences. This, also, would affect the profits to be made by the Trust. Japan was told, in 1991 and 1992, if they chose not to go along with this plan, there would be a major disaster to Japan and this would then cause a major global effect. A white paper has been completed and positioned with certain law offices to be filed with the International courts and U.S. Congressional Leaders in the event any tragic accidents should occur to the principals of the Trust. This notice of a white paper has also been filed with the Japanese Government. Both governments are fully aware of these Securities, as this writer has personally met representatives of the U.S. State Department and U.S. Treasury.

Most Zaibatsu chiefs were university graduates with degrees in economics. In 1924, the U.S. Government filed suit in New York to recover 2.5 million dollars in wartime overpayments to Mitsui's Standard Aircraft Corporation. At the hearings, sensational charges and accusations were made against Mitsui. A U.S. senator had released his report to the Justice Department accusing the Mitsui's companies of exerting indirect but powerful influence in the U.S. This influence extended to Congress and many departments of the U.S. Government. Mitsui had on their payroll attorneys and politicians who were attempting to run roughshod over the U.S. Government and the taxpayers. (7) The most damaging testimony in this case was not able to be substantiated.

Japan's Foreign Minister, Tanaka, convened the Eastern Regions Conference, which was held in the summer of 1927. Top level cabinet members, political leaders, Zaibatsu and many well known Japanese economical experts attended. No report was ever issued from this convention, but in essence it was postulated that vital rights of Manchuria and Mongolia would become part of Japan's economic development and security. Japan's necessity to conquer all of China was to protect Japan's rights in the inevitability of eventual war with the United States and Great Britain. This alliance was to be known as the "Tanaka Program." (8)

Post War 1945 to 1952

On September 2, 1945, Foreign Minister Shgemitsu Mamoru, representing Japan, signed the unconditional surrender documents with General Douglas MacArthur, representing the United States and its allies. General MacArthur, the Supreme Commander of Japan's occupation forces began immediately to carry out the policies set forth in his instructions from President Truman. His instructions were to disarm, demilitarize, and return overseas portions of Japan's empire to its former owners. General MacArthur was to remove any and all obstacles for development of a democratic society, and foster a free economy for an adequate peaceful existence. The General decided that Japan should retain its own government for routine administration, and help execute orders from SCAP (Supreme Commander for Allied Powers). At this point of time, Shibusawa Keizo was the Finance Minister, as well as being an officer and a large shareholder in numerous Zaibatsu controlled companies including the Teikoku Bank of Japan (the merger of Mitsui and Dai-Ichi Banks).

On September 22, 1945, SCAP decreed orders to break up the Zaibatus, and prevent their revival. This meant the break up of the four largest companies: Mitsui, Mitsubishi, Sumitomo and Yasuda. Zaibatsu leaders, not given a chance to cultivate influence with SCAP, turned to the foreign press. Their statement was that the old Zaibatsu did not profit from the war, only the new Zaibatsu. Mitsui made contact with Colonel Raymond C. Kramer, who headed SCAP's economic and scientific section in charge of the Zaibatsu dissolution. Colonel Kramer was not unsympathetic, as he had past dealings with Mitsui. Before Zaibatsu could make any further moves, the military police, on October 8, 1945, took securities from Mitsui headquarters, valued at 1,200,000,000 Yen (about 281 million dollars at the prewar rate of .2343 per Yen), and from Mitsubishi's headquarters, approximately 50,000,000 Yen. The impounded Securities were stored in vaults of the non-Zaibatsu Hypothec Bank pending disposition.

As of 1945, the ten largest Zaibatsu controlled companies accounted for about thirty-five percent of Japan's paid up capital, fifty-five percent of bank assets, seventy-one percent of loans and advances, and sixty-seven percent of the Trust bank deposits. They also controlled seventy-five percent of non-life and thirty-six percent of life insurance assets. These ten largest Zaibatsu controlled companies had estimated assets of thirty billion U.S. dollars. Their banks accounted for fifty percent of deposits, sixty-five percent of outstanding loans of all private banks, twenty-five percent of all corporate and partnership capital, and thirty-three percent of the capital in heavy industry. (9)

Mitsui, in 1945, was probably the world's largest private business organization, with the control of an estimated three hundred and thirty-six companies. It was estimated that Mitsui employed one-point-eight million people in Japan and one million overseas. The Big Four Zaibatsu Group devised a plan to save their companies, and on November 6, 1945, their plan was presented to SCAP and accepted. SCAP issued instructions to the Imperial Japanese Government to prohibit sale, gift, assignment, or transfer of any property including securities. The Japanese Government directed its politicians to prepare plans for the dissolution of other monopolistic businesses.

It may be asked how the Japanese were entrusted with such incompatible responsibilities. During the early period after World War II, Japanese authorities gathered among the London circle of English speaking businessman, and with just about anyone with experience in overseas trading, and with banks. By mingling with these businessmen, they developed channels of influence with the Americans. Friendships were developed between the two, with the intent by the Japanese to meet all their friends and many former associates, including London's finest, Downing Street's best, and of course, anyone that was well known by the U.S. State Department's leading members. It was not very long before the Japanese were able to determine the weakest point in SCAP's armor, as well as Japan's strongest hold. This was the rivalry between new dealers and conservatives who intended to build up Japan, with the help of the business community as a bulwark against Communism. SCAP's G2 section (Intelligence) General, Charles A. Willoughby, was more concerned with encountering radicalism and Soviet influence, and so he helped to advance the cause of his friends in the economic world. The support given to Zaibatsu by early Cabinet members (Japan) was very financial, especially when defeat was certain. Japanese legislation was approved to indemnify munitions manufacturers for wartime losses. Immediately after Japan's surrender, funds were dispersed by raiding the treasury, of which eighteen billion Yen was paid out. In November 1945, SCAP became aware of his financial rape and prohibited any further pay out; however, under pretext, reimbursements were made into blocked accounts until August 1946. These additional funds totaled fifty-four billion Yen. (10)

As SCAP investigated, they found companies hoarding huge amounts of scarce materials in anticipation of Japan's defeat, which was estimated at one-hundred-fifty billion Yen. These exposures prompted SCAP, in 1946, to eliminate from businesses, all persons who held high positions since 1937 in industry, finance, commerce or agriculture; they were to be purged. The purge swept out 220,000 leaders. SCAP, at wits end, to unravel the tangled scheme of Japanese society and enforce regulations were either resisted, evaded, or ignored. SCAP had neither the resources nor the will to save the Japanese from all SCAP greed and folly and, at the end of 1947, Japanese Government subsidies and American handouts ended. Many of SCAP occupation officials used SCAP authority to export securities, real estate, and works of art from Japanese owners who were reduced to desperation by the freeze on securities and bank accounts. Many went into partnership with local businessmen and quite a few of these carpetbaggers were American lawyers, who are now millionaires or billionaires and still live in Japan to this present time. (11)

MacArthur vowed in 1945 to breakup Zaibatsu. The Chinese Nationalists demanded Japanese factories as reparations for factories taken by the USSR, and the Australian, British, and the USSR also all wanted reparations. If they succeeded, Japan's industry would be destroyed. MacArthur announced no reparations, but the United States would provide assistance. Thus, under the new constitution, it saved the essential political and economic system of prewar Japan, which was signed on November 3, 1946, and the enforcement date was set for May 3, 1947. On July 3, 1947, SCAP ordered _ dissolution of Mitsui and Mitsubishi, which was a shock to all people concerned, including Capitol Hill. The U.S. politicians knew nothing about the termination of these two major Japanese companies. This meant dissolving all of their general trading companies worldwide with immense pressure applied by the occupation.

Banking the anti-reform forces were many American businessmen who sympathized with Zaibatsu. Leading American banks and corporations had capital and business ties of long standing with Japanese firms, which in 1941, had held seventy-five percent of all direct foreign investments (100 million dollars) in Japan with General Electric being the largest investor. American creditors and investors were anxious to recover their investments, including interest, dividends, and overdue licensing fees, which came to a grand total of four-hundred-million dollars. These creditors were lobbying vigorously against Japanese economic reform in Washington with their argument and defense being the bulwark against Communism. They really wanted to protect their current investments and future investments. The first barrage began in the U.S. in December of 1947. Their complaint was that Japan was costing the American taxpayer millions of dollars each year and, concluded by saying, Japan would be a most attractive prospect for investment of U.S. private industry capital. (12)

In March, 1948, Under-Secretary of the Army, William H. Draper, was sent to Japan to initiate changes in U.S. policy. Draper was a former (and future) vice president of the Dillion, Read & Company, a leading Wall Street investment company. He headed the economic division of the American military in Germany, after which he helped to reverse occupation, anti-monopoly programs there by preparing the way for reviving German Trusts. Draper and his firm had close ties to the Rockefellers and other major groups in developing overseas resources and industries. This group was the leading brain power to the Truman administration. Draper was particularly interested in a prewar investment (two million dollars) in Daido Power Company. Draper's self serving interest was killing two birds with one stone. Accompanying Draper on this adventure was Percy H. Johnson, Chairman of Chemical Bank and Trust, N.Y., which had close ties with Mitsui Bank. The Draper-Johnson Committee reported to the U.S. War Department on April 26, 1948. They called for sharp cuts in reparations (eventually cut by 75 percent), and for the U.S. to provide initial imported material. By year's end, the U.S. provided four-hundred-million dollars in aid. MacArthur, to justify his performance, asked for an investigation, which started in May of 1948. The roll of the five man group was obviously to whitewash what was left of the Zaibatsu establishment. One member, a paid agent of Zaibatsu, was W. R. Hutchinson, a lawyer (former special assistant to the U.S. Attorney General). Hutchinson offered his services to change the policy of U.S. compensation. Generous, he was not, as he directed his work only to satisfy his private clients. (13)

At the end of the war there were 325 (Zaibatsu) operating companies, forty-two of them now were being or have been dissolved. Still in tact, was the largest bank, Teikoku (later dissolved into its original components, Mitsui and Dai-lchi banks).

Early in 1951, Iohn Foster Dulles, was appointed by President Truman to visit Japan concerning terms of the peace treaty. Accompanying Mr.

Dulles was John D. Rockefeller III, Controller of Chase Manhattan Bank and Standard Oil Empire. These two companies were emerging as the largest foreign investor in post war Japan. The Peace Treaty was finally signed on September 8, 1951. During this time, the Korean Conflict started and the U.S. needed Japan for armament, which in turn was the avenue for placing Japan back on its economic feet.

Spilled water can never be returned to its original vessel, the Zaibatsu elders had solemnly declared after the trust-busters finished their work. This was true only in the narrow sense of ownership. Incredibly, the new wine of postwar economic liberation found its way into the same old bottles filling them almost precisely to the brim.

In 1951, the U.S. was encouraging American corporations to share technology with Japan; one case in point was the patent rights with Dupont for Nylon 66. In 1952, more than ninety-five percent of trading capital consisted of borrowing. The ratio of owned capital seldom rose above ten percent. Frustrating American trust-busters, the Zaibatsu banks served as instruments for reviving oligopoly.

In 1953, RCA, Westinghouse, Dupont, Armco Steel, and General Electric sold patents to the Japanese and helped the start-up of its factories. This prompted Fortune magazine to ask, "Is it in the long-term interest of the United States? Will not revitalizing Japan's industries cut into U.S. markets abroad and increasingly invade our domestic market?" (14)

In 1953, the vision was there, but all of the U.S. politicians wore blinders. Who said the future could not be predicted. Douglas MacArthur was well aware of the competitive advantage inherent in the Japanese approach to work. In 1951, MacArthur warned that Japanese veneration of work could eventually propel Japan forward against Americans consumed with the desire for less work and more luxury. (15)

In the 1960's, Japan's miraculous emergence proved to be a first rate economic power, yet very little literature provides a creditable explanation of how they arrived at that level or by whom. One source was Kobayashi, President of the Development Bank, who became custodian of the Untied States Aid Counterpart Fund, which terminated in 1953 after amassing more than eight-hundred-million dollars from the sale of U.S. Aid Commodities. In 1960, President Eisenhower was to visit Japan. Hanging in the balance were World Bank loans of one-hundred-million dollars, Export-Import Bank of forty-million, Japan's Arabian Oil Company of one-hundred-million and numerous industrial loans, floating Bonds, and so forth. Also pending was Japan's two-billion-dollar debt for post war aid, and the United States was in a position either to demand payment in full or to reduce the amount drastically. Eisenhower's visit was canceled due to protests by the Communists.

Also, during the 1960's, Japan exports rose seventeen percent a year. Japan's extra income estimated a billion dollars a year from 1966 through 1972. (16)

Japan's favorable balance of trade, which averaged less than four-hundred-million dollars a year since 1960, leaped to an average of 2.725 billion a year in the 1967-1970 period and to 7.787 billion in 1971. This surplus, and foreign exchange reserves accumulation, changed Japan from a debtor to a creditor nation and one of the world's biggest international lenders and investors.

In 1959, Thomas Dewey, an unsuccessful Republican candidate for the President, was retained by JETRO (Japan External Trade Organization) as its representative in the United States. Dewey's law firm represented Lawrence Rockefeller and American Telephone and Telegraph, and was to receive fees and expenses reported as two-hundred-thousand a year for being Japan's watchdog (Dewey was an experienced lobbyist). In 1960, Dewey's political protege, Richard M. Nixon, who had served as vice-president under Eisenhower, devoted most of his time to clients of his own law firm such as PEPSICO, and MITSUI & Co. U.S.A., Inc. In April 1964, Nixon visited Japan and met with government heads of state. Although Dewey gave the impression of neglecting his duties, Nixon promoted the Japanese – United States trade and business relations energetically, visiting Tokyo at least once a year until he ran for President of the United States. It is probably impossible to learn precisely what benefits JETRO derived from its employment of Dewey or Mitsui from Nixon's services. However, it can be deduced that the fees they paid were not wasted. Dewey, Nixon's political godfather, was the third man in a republican triumvirate with John Foster Dulles and Winthrop Aldrich, brother-in-law of John D. Rockefeller and Chairman of . Chase Manhattan Bank. Dewey's early financial backer had been C. Douglas Dillon, who controlled most of the voting stock in Dillon, Read & Company. Dillon became Secretary of the Treasury under Kennedy, and Dean Rusk left the presidency of the Rockefeller Foundation for a spot in the State Department, thus both Dewey and Nixon seem to have been ensconce din the upper echelons of the American's "Zaibutsu" concerns most interested in the Japanese economy. (17)

In 1972, Nixon signed over Okinawa to the Japanese government. Japan had long negotiated for the return of its island, which included all of the infrastructure repaired and in good order, and paid for by the United States. An executive with Daiwa, Japan's second biggest securities house, frames the issue bluntly, "It is one thing to compete for a share of the automobile market, but it is quite another to compete on the financial battleground. Money is the blood that runs through every economy, carrying food to the nation's brain and heart. There are those who will see competition in the field of finance as competition for the control of the body's bloodstream. I am one of those people." (18)

Summary Funds

On September 2, 1945, Japan surrendered. MacArthur had orders to restore Japan, and his decision was that the United States will not allow reparations by other countries, and that the United States would supply all the funds.

On October 8, 1945, the United States Army took Securities from Mitsui valued at two-hundred and eighty-one million dollars, and fifty million Yen from Mitsubishi, which was stored in the vaults of the non-Zaibatsu Hypothec Bank.

The Development Bank custodian of the United States Aid Counterpart Fund amassed more than eight-hundred-million dollars, which was terminated in 1953.

The United States post war aid amounted to two billion dollars and was not repaid as of 1960. The United States made vast improvements to Okinawa and the island was turned over to Japan in 1972 by Nixon.

This very brief description of Japan and its culture, as well as its strong influence in the world, is important to understand before one can understand the following chapters of the secret MacArthur fund and its current role in the United States of America and Japan.

My role, as stated in the beginning, is a messenger of sorts, and I am presently involved in structuring an international banking system and a development system that will be the foundation for utilizing the securities discussed in this book.

I have tried to explain my beginning role working for a company on the international scene, which in time led me to the Trust, and I do not know if it is destiny or just luck, or maybe, perhaps, disaster. In any event, it changed my life completely: my outlook, my conditions, and my complete indifference to the total monetary values, which have been retooled to see only the task at hand.

Notes

1. Nihon Shoki (Chronicles of Japan).
2. Prime Minister Yasuhiro Nakasone, Speech to the Diet, December 1984.
3. Japan's War by Edwin P. Hoyt, 1986.
4. The Rise and Development of Japan's Modern Economy, 1969.
5. The Japanese and Sun Yat-Sen, 1954.
6. Estimated Study by Taskahashi. Quoted in Tsuchiya Mitsui Zaibatsu no. 1 Hatten P. 26.
7. Quoted from Russell, House of Mitsui, P 239
8. Eto Shinkichi, The Proposed Laterception of the South Manchurian Rai l road, Acts Asiatica # 14, 1969, P 59.
9. Two Aibatsu Dissolutions, 1954.
10. Two Aibatsu Dissolutions, 1954.
11. Arita Kyosuke Sogo Shosha (General Trading Co.) Tokyo Nihon Keizai Shimbun-Shaw, 1970, P 53.
12. Quoted from Hadley, Antitrust in Japan, PP 135-36.
13. Edo Hideo Book, Sushiya No Shomon and Three Centuries of Japanese Business, Chapter 26, P 394.
14. Fortune, April 1953, P 188.
15. David Halberstam, The Rechoning (N.Y. William Morrow &; Co.), 1986, P 115.
16. Kuristo Shimbtun, March 3, 1973, Quoted from the Japan Times, March 23, 1973.
17. Three Centuries of Japanese Business.
18. Yen, by Daniel Burstein, Introduction, P 28.

P.O.BOX 15288 WEST PALM BEACH
FLORIDA 33416-5288

CERTIFIED. P 192 938 777

DEPARTMENT OF THE TREASURY
UNITED STATES CUSTOM SERVICE

COMMISSIONER OF CUSTOMS
Att.Currency transportation report
Washington D.C. 20229.

Nov.23,1990.
West Palm Beach,
Florida.

Gentlemen:

As to enclosed documentation,
MR.MOBLEY,Harold,Gene,
Born:02/05/28
USA Passport:P 011052603
USA Address:3855 Bower Rd.S.W.
Roanoke Virginia,24018
On behalf of: COMPLEX INDUSTRIES HOLDINGS LTD.
            P.O.BOX 15288
            WEST PALM BEACH,FL 33416-5288

transports NON BEARER SECURITIES,(in japanese yen)
to Tokyo,Japan,
Total value in US Dollars,under today exchange rate
approx of US$ 3.5 billion.(Three and half billion US Dollars),
whereby Mr.Mobley will leave to TOKYO,

as to following schedule:

CONTINENTAL AIRLINE NO.451 25 NOV. WEST PALM BEACH-HOUSTON
CONTINENTAL AIRLINE NO.4139 25 NOV. HOUSTON-TOKYO.

Remarks:

The same securities have been imported into USA and filed as to
attached copies,from which will be transported by Mr.Mobley only
a part of them.(In form of copies are attached thereto).

Under penalty of perjury,I declare,that this report has been
examined by me and to the best of my knowledge and belief it is
true,correct and complete.

Sincerely Yours,

Dr.Sandor Mihaly,Chairman and President
Complex Industries Holdings Ltd.
P.O.Box 15288,West Palm Beach,Fl 33416-5288

NOV 23 1990
DR. SANDOR MIHALY
PRESIDENT
CI HOLDINGS LTD.

TOTAL OF
15 SHEETS.

G E N E R A L   R E P O R T

LATEST IMPORTS

Number   890427

April 27, 1989
Page one

Latest imports of Complex Industries Holdings Ltd.

"E1"   Report number 33-CNA 890429-A. Yen denominated financial
              instruments of approximately five billion USD to be brought
(Import)   back into the USA on April 29, 1989 BECAUSE JAPANESE
              POLITICAL TURMOIL REQUIRES DELAY IN PROCESSING. Report filed
              with US Commissioner of Customs Washington D.C. on April 28,
              1989 by Certified mail P 060 111 526.

"E2"   Report number 33-CN 890429-B. Yen denominated financial
              instruments of approximately one billion five hundred sixty
(Import)   five million USD returned to USA on April 29, 1989 BECAUSE
              JAPANESE POLITICAL TURMOIL REQUIRES DELAY IN PROCESSING.
              Reported to US Commissioner of Customs Washington D.C. by
              Certified mail P 060 111 526 on April 28, 1989.

"E3"   Report number 33-CNC 890429-C. Yen denominated financial
              instruments of approximately five billion USD brought to USA
(Import)   on April 29, 1989 BECAUSE JAPANESE POLITICAL TURMOIL REQUIRES
              DELAY IN PROCESSING. Reported to US Commissioner of Customs
              Washington D.C. by Certified mail P 060 111 526 on April 28,
              1989. FIRST ENTRY INTO USA UNDER THE DIRECTION OF COMPLEX
              INDUSTRIES HOLDINGS LTD.

S U M M A R Y

Estimated USD amount Report number 33-CNA 890429 A   = $ 5,000,000,000.-- **
Estimated USD amount Report number 33-CN 890429 B   = $ 1,565,000,000.-- **
Estimated USD amount Report number 33-CNC 890429 C   = $ 5,000,000,000.-- **
Estimated total USD amount for all three Reports   = $11,565,000,000.-- **
Estimated USD amount for earned interest **   = $ 4,435,000,000.-- **
Estimated USD total amount for Principal & Interest = $16,000,000,000.-- **

**These estimated amounts are depending on the present exchange rate of the
  yen and the U.S. dollar.

Complex Industries Holdings Ltd.

Dr. Sandor Mihaly
President

NOV 2 3 1990

DR. SANDOR MIHALY
PRESIDENT
CI HOLDINGS LTD.

107

DEPARTMENT OF THE TREASURY
UNITED STATES CUSTOMS SERVICE

REPORT OF INTERNATIONAL TRANSPORTATION OF CURRENCY OR MONETARY INSTRUMENTS

Form Approved
OMB No. 1515-0013
This form is to be filed with the United States Customs Service

Privacy Act Notification on reverse

Customs Use Only

Control No.
31 USC 5316; 31 CFR 103.23 and 103.25
Please Type or Print

PART I - FOR INDIVIDUAL DEPARTING FROM OR ENTERING THE UNITED STATES

1. NAME (Last or family, first and middle)
2. IDENTIFYING NO. (See Instructions)
3. DATE OF BIRTH (Mo./Day/Yr.)
02 05 28

4. PERMANENT ADDRESS IN UNITED STATES OR ABROAD
P.O. Box 15580 Newport Beach, California 92658

5. OF WHAT COUNTRY ARE YOU A CITIZEN/SUBJECT?
USA

6. ADDRESS WHILE IN THE UNITED STATES
same as above

7. PASSPORT NO. & COUNTRY
(USA)

8. U.S. VISA DATE
9. PLACE UNITED STATES VISA WAS ISSUED
10. IMMIGRATION ALIEN NO. (if any)

11. CURRENCY OR MONETARY INSTRUMENT WAS: (Complete 11A or 11B)

A. EXPORTED		B. IMPORTED	
Departed From: (City in U.S.)	Arrived At: (Foreign City/Country)	From: (Foreign City/Country) Tokyo, Japan	At: (City in U.S.) Los Angeles, Ca

PART II - FOR PERSON SHIPPING MAILING OR RECEIVING CURRENCY OR MONETARY INSTRUMENTS

12. NAME (Last or family, first and middle)
13. IDENTIFYING NO. (See Instructions)
14. DATE OF BIRTH (Mo./Da/Yr.)

15. PERMANENT ADDRESS IN UNITED STATES OR ABROAD
725 Market Street Wilmington, Delaware

16. OF WHAT COUNTRY ARE YOU A CITIZEN/SUBJECT?

17. ADDRESS WHILE IN THE UNITED STATES
P.O. Box 15580 Newport Beach, California 92659

18. PASSPORT NO. & COUNTRY

19. U.S. VISA DATE
20. PLACE UNITED STATES VISA WAS ISSUED
21. IMMIGRATION ALIEN NO. (if any)

22. CURRENCY OR MONETARY INSTRUMENTS DATE SHIPPED
Apr. ,89
DATE RECEIVED
Apr. 29,89

23. CURRENCY OR MONETARY INSTRUMENTS
☐ Shipped To
[X] Received From

NAME AND ADDRESS
Complex Industries Holdings Ltd
see (15) (17) above
JAPANESE POLITICAL TURMOIL
REQUIRES DELAY IN PROCESSING
(see attach report nbr. 89042/)

24. IF THE CURRENCY OR MONETARY INSTRUMENT WAS MAILED, SHIPPED, OR TRANSPORTED COMPLETE BLOCKS A AND B.
A. Method of Shipment (Auto, U.S. Mail, Public Carrier, etc.)
Courier of
B. Name of Transporter/Carrier
(1) above on Japan Air #62

PART III - CURRENCY AND MONETARY INSTRUMENT INFORMATION (SEE INSTRUCTIONS ON REVERSE.) (To be completed by everyone)

25. TYPE AND AMOUNT OF CURRENCY/MONETARY INSTRUMENTS

Coins .... ☐ A. ▶ $
Currency .... ☐ B. ▶
Other (such as Sheets etc.) Financial Instruments ☐ C. ▶ $ Aprox one billion five hundred
Issued in Japanese yen currency — sixty five million USD value

(Add lines A, B and C)
TOTAL AMOUNT $1,565,000,000.--

Value in U.S. Dollars

26. IF OTHER THAN U.S. CURRENCY IS INVOLVED, PLEASE COMPLETE BLOCKS A AND B. (SEE SPECIAL INSTRUCTIONS)
A. Currency Name
yen
B. Country
Japan

PART IV - GENERAL - TO BE COMPLETED BY ALL TRAVELERS, SHIPPERS AND RECIPIENTS

27. WERE YOU ACTING AS AN AGENT, ATTORNEY OR IN CAPACITY FOR ANYONE IN THIS CURRENCY OR MONETARY INSTRUMENT ACTIVITY? (If "Yes" complete A, B and C) ☐ Yes ☐ No

PERSON IN WHOSE BEHALF YOU ARE ACTING ▶
A. Name
B. Address
PO BOX 15580 Newport Beach, Calif. 92659
C. Business activity occupation or profession
Research
Engineering
Financing

I declare penalties of perjury, I declare that I have examined this report, and to the best of my knowledge and belief it is true, correct and complete.

28. NAME AND TITLE
Dr.
29. SIGNATURE
30. DATE
Apr. 27, 89

(Replaces IRS Form 4790 which is obsolete)

Customs Form 4790 (120384)

□ 普通預金証書

受領権者
氏名　桑原　信孝　彦坂　公夫　様

口座番号　5820123

還付金額
¥9,990,000,000.-

支払開始年月日　昭和58年1月18日　　振出日　昭和57年12月21日

上記の還付金は、本証裏面記載の支払期日に本証持参人に対し
お支払いします。

株式会社　**第一勧業銀行**
京都支店

◇特殊預金◇　　※本証の譲渡貿入を禁じます。

A第6083号　□普通預金証書

受領権者
氏名　桑原　信孝　彦坂　公夫　様

口座番号　5820123

還付金額
¥9,990,000,000.-

支払開始年月日　昭和58年1月18日　　振出日　昭和57年12月21日

上記の還付金は、本証裏面記載の支払期日に本証持参人に対し
お支払いします。

株式会社　**第一勧業銀行**
京都支店

◇特殊預金◇　　※本証の譲渡貿入を禁じます。

A第6084号　□普通預金証書

受領権者
氏名　桑原　信孝　彦坂　公夫　様

口座番号　5820123

還付金額
¥9,990,000,000.-

支払開始年月日　昭和58年1月18日　　振出日　昭和57年12月21日

上記の還付金は、本証裏面記載の支払期日に本証持参人に対し
お支払いします。

株式会社　**第一勧業銀行**
京都支店

◇特殊預金◇　　※本証の譲渡貿入を禁じます。

NOV 23 1990

DR. SANDOR MIHALY
PRESIDENT

CI HOLDINGS LTD.

Informing Japanese Minister of Finance

On November 19, 1990, the following letter was sent by the Doctor and the Trust to the Minister of Finance (MOF) in Japan outlining the objective of the Trust, the historical background of the Yen Securities, and the benefit to Japan and the United States of America. It is written, unedited for grammar, in the Doctor's own words.

General Evaluation
November 29, 1990

Subject:
Yen Securities (hereinafter "Financial Instruments"), dismissed as counterfeit by Deputy Director at Ministry of Finance, Japan, at Government Debt Division, Finance Bureau (hereinafter "MOF").
*****

Gentlemen:

Khrushchev delivered the model of Sputnik to the table of President Kennedy at the time when the U.S. had no satellite yet. Until that time and after for nearly one quarter of century the USA taxpayers spent trillion and trillion dollars among others also for the defense of Japan.

As interesting historical contradiction is – due to prohibition after the lost World War II, Japan was not allowed to build up military establishment, instead Japan has built up until today, tremendous great industrial and financial world-wide extended admirable power.

However, Japanese nowadays traveling to USA and realize that in USA the common worker has much more comfortable homes, circumstances, than the Japanese at home, regardless from their great international financial power.

Japan, today is a very much contradictory miracle. In one hand she is global power, in other hand most part of the country looks like as an underdeveloped area.

This fact creates a nucleus for social political explosions, what LDP (Liberal Democratic Party) cannot sustain, unless will be eliminated above unbalance.

***

What to do anything all of this time with the above "subject?" Itself

111

the referred financial instruments were in hands of very amateurish people, whose skill and political education did not reach the level for deeper understanding, that talking about international politics and can be triggered international repercussions, if the referred financial instruments will be used improperly and unprofessionally.

What is the interest of Japan and what is the involvement of USA, regarding these financial instruments? This funny question has very deep historical root. Practical point of view MOF can declare privately that the financial instruments are counterfeit and never have been issued. However, the present, legitimate holder of the CD's, the Trust do not need to prove that the CD's are genuine. MOF (Minister of Finance) must furnish the prove that the CD's are counterfeit. 1

The people of MOF are servants of the government and they following the received instructions. However they well understand, that this instruments are in amateurish hands lethal economic and political weapon against Japan. This is why they are stating that there are counterfeit.

Upon unilateral declaration and threat by one or more of the officers of MOF the brokers, middle man, naive business people in once abandoning further "try," however continuously arriving newcomers, repeating the same.

So during the past several years has been proliferated the actions world-wide to "make big monies" on the financial instruments by this amateurs, all of them on some way approached the same place of MOF. Of course, cannot be blamed the officers of MOF for their "Declarations."

The turning point occurred concerning this above outlined trend, when have been accumulated this instruments in the safe of, in Europe based, very sophisticated, we can say, Trust, under management of the writer of his memo.

It is highly probably, that at top level no one has the complete and accurate detailed information, what is the program of the Trust and what would be the final outcome, if the trust would chose the co-called European Alternative Program (EAP).

I believe, however, that in Japan at top level are inaccurate notions about the organization, headed by the Doctor. Must be emphasized, that the Trust made all necessary legal research concerning the history of the referred financial instruments, which going back to the end of the

World War II to the period of MacArthur, who worked out the Japanese constitution together with late Emperor Hirohito.

The so-called "Secret Funds" which served as financial source for the buildup of the democratic Japan has been turned over to Japanese hands later on by former President Nixon in conjunction with the Peace Treaty.

It is not the subject of the Trust actions to evaluate whether or not the actions by President Nixon can be legally supported, even in retrospect, or it was some kind of different qualifiable political maneuver.

Our function is, due to the fact that for some, by not us selected reason, we have the destiny to resolve this historical puzzle and place in the books of the history, revising certain already written chapters.

Our motives only in very minor degree driven by desire for money. Of course, we are working, as Capitalistic system used to be for very modest fee.

The Chief motive is to fulfill our historical mission, to manage under tight control the distorted, potentially explosive system and the financial instruments and their economic values deliver-back to the place where originally belong.

The existence of the Communist system, in essence, the USSR as Super Power, was the only threat for the Trust to loosing the control about EAP one year ago. It was in that time greater risk, that the financial instruments will be taken over by hostile forces.

Today, above danger does not exist any more.

Under the "New World Order" did remain only one superpower, which is today already historical fact and no one argue any more about this sentence.

The unprecedented UNO actions, among the today expected resolution is the prove, that only USA is in the position to manage the balance on the entire world, for the benefit and security of all nations. This request the highest level of responsible decisions, actions and leadership.

The US Government and the Legislative Body (Congress) working together so closely, which never happened during the past few decades in the US history.

All of this what to do anything with the subject financial instruments?

With patience, it can be understood,

∗∗∗

The Trust has completed documentation, based on legal research, made by widely know international exports – concerning the origin of the referred financial instruments. By historical (not yet legal terms) can be furnished unrejectable prove, that the financial instruments represent a long range investment of the US taxpayers, done by historical channels and during a historical period.

The issue is not whether or not the financial instruments are counterfeit (there are genuine), the issue is: What would be the effect to the international political scene, if all questions and answers, relating with M-Funds would go to the international political arena?

The recruit scandal is the prove, that identical origin of financial instruments in amateurish hands how dangerous can be. The Trust will not trigger "recruit scandal" or similar phenomena. The Trust has the function under the laws in and outside of USA to provide facilities and accommodation to resolve this problem definitively.

We have no intention to do favor for the Japanese government, we are not threatening anybody. We are acting responsible and for the interest of USA, consequently for the interest of Japan, too.

We do not have any authorization from the US government. We do not need any authorization from any one.

We are protected under the Constitution of the USA and all of our actions has been and will be executed under the Laws and Regulations,

This is why we do not need to hide anything.

∗∗∗

In order to present convincing evidence for top level people in Japan, they must be approached by intellectual methods furnishing the proof that our proposal is genuine and workable, and can be kept under restricted control without any wide and malicious publicity, avoiding all unexperienced and some time unscrupulous brokers.

I outline below in very short terms the so called European Alternative Program in order to convince the proper high level, that the already structured "Ready to Proceed" mechanism, which can be in very much details presented by my representative bank officer, is the best solution.

∗∗∗

114

In contrast of, by representative represented mechanics, does exist an alternative program, European Alternative Program (EAP) which is undesirable, however, also workable and has been entirely prepared to proceed in case, may be, the first alternative for some illogical reason will not be accept. It is know, that in Haag exist the International Court, which has no real jurisdiction about any country. The effect of any decision of theirs is rather political declaration, that real verdict, and then cannot be enforced.

However, the international publicity, relating with public hearings, perhaps much more powerful tool in this case, than can be thought.

It is so, that even if some of the representatives of the Japanese Government would be requested to appear before the court as witness, they not necessarily would appear in Haag.

However, the trust has the legal power, based on documentation, that the US Government will consider to send its witness to the International court. .

Of course, knowing this factor, the same claim, to be presented at the Haag Court simultaneously will be filed also in Japan at the proper court, requesting the Japanese Government the verification of the genuineness of the financial instruments.

Therefore in Haag, before the International Court will be publicized the same documents, like in Japan at the Japanese Court. this can be achieved very easy, since the constitution in Japan has been drafted based on the US Constitution. the experts who already reviewed the case have not seen any problems about the parallel and simultaneous court procedure in Haag and Tokyo, consequently also in Washington.

It is great deal of naivety to believe that Japan Government is in the position under above mentioned conditions refuse to delegate the witness at Tokyo Court.

If we assume, that some extreme Japanese Group, terrorist, etc., want to kill all persons who managing and assisting this process from side of the Trust, they will not reach the desired result. Cannot be silenced any more the efficiently of the actions anymore, because any, above referred hostile act immediately will trigger the release in different countries already existing complete documentation which will trigger the EAP automatically.

If we assume, that the Doctor will be assassinated, perhaps would be a nice funeral, however, would not change anything regarding the end effect of EAP.

EAP will start with full publicity and the extract of the files will appear in all major capitals in the first page at the most known daily news papers. The EAP would trigger, first of all in Japan the greatest internal political repercussion. Two years ago, before Gorbachev gained his full power, would have been to risky to trigger the EAP, because perhaps Japan would have fallen into the interest sphere of Stalinist type of USSR by help of far leftist communist powers in and outside of Japan.

(Talking about nearly 600 billion dollars value of issued and genuine, existing, controlled instruments, which in essence belong – legally can be proven only by the Trust - to the American taxpayers.)

EAP of course would have very much support from both of the two parties in USA. The Trust relating fees also will be justified and no one will object them.

Our strength is our rationality and objectivity.

If the financial instruments will be confirmed openly as genuine (based on the EAP) would mean, that the trade surplus of Japan would disappear from one hour to the other one. The exponentially. The American industry, business community would applaud to the Trust and only the Japanese population will suffer. This scenario is undesirable.

Japan is member of IMF, World Bank and many other international bodies and treaties bids Japan on the international arena, therefore EAP will work and very quickly.

The Trust has the best and well known international experts whose witness stand would force out the truth and all documents and past events will be able documented.

Who will be blamed?

It is not our function to determine.

***

I want to make a statement here in writing. Has been recorded by tape a life threat against Doctor some time ago. Today I am still alive. The lift threat is the proof that the system built up by me is genuine workable and will be successful.

The EAP do not need to use. The most genuine procedure already has been structures and my representative can present in all details.

***

EPILOGUE TO CHAPTER SIX
EVALUATION

The constructor of this "Evaluation" is a man with minimal life requirements; his destiny to build up in the field of medicine an entire new system to prepare the medical sciences for the new challenges in the next century for the benefit of our children, as well as for the benefit of other peoples children and for the benefit of the whole of humanity, regardless of race, color, or belonging.

I really do hope that my representative will have the chance to present the concrete program at top level without delay.

Dr. Sandor Mihaly, Chairman, The Swiss Trust

The above letter was sent to the Minister of Finance in Japan and, as of that date, November 29, 1990, all work has been on hold due to the serious problems of the recession in Japan. The basic problem is the excesses that have occurred in the U.S.A. during the last twenty-odd years, and the cleansing of the criminal elements in Japan. This will probably take the balance of the 1990's to be completed.

Since the November 29, 1990 letter, which was sent to MOF, Japan, a few more Yen Securities keep popping up by people who think that they can use these instruments as collateral, or attempt to cash them in. One such case came up in Tampa, Florida, in 1992 where people attempted to use these instruments at a well known brokerage house as collateral. These people were picked up by the authorities for attempting to use foreign securities illegally. The U.S. Attorney, along with the Secret Service, requested the assistance of the Chairman on what course they should take as he is the expert. They were told that any attempt to go to Japan would be foolish and would result in nothing, as Japan would not disclose any information concerning the notes. In fact, they would be politely handled and the end result would be wasted time and could be a stab in the back. Later the U.S. Government formally requested from Japan a representative to testify at a trial in Tampa as to the authenticity of the Securities. Japan refused the U.S. request. The

U.S. is no man's land. The only action that the U.S. can take is to find someone that can testify on the status of the notes. There is one person, in hiding, and any attempt to bring him out would result in his death before he could be delivered to testify. This is an example of Japan's ability, its "way of strategy," in handling certain situations.

The U.S. Federal counterfeit charges were dismissed without explanation in Tampa, Florida (Tampa Tribune, December 7, 1995).

This final signing over of the U.S. aid and reparation amounts to the political nationalists personally by Nixon, happened at the time Vice-President Nixon was running for the Presidential office.

The last chain of events triggered the personal wealth of many business political leaders of Japan, who had already misused these funds, as well as undoubtedly, a few American politicians. The past subject has been well known to the U.S.A. by some of the political leaders, major law offices, and U.S. government agencies. It was, and still is, a very well kept secret from the U.S. citizen as well as the average Japanese citizen. As of now, the Japanese people and the American people believe that all the past Japanese reparations were handled properly and settled in the proper legal way. Little does the U.S. and Japanese citizen know that control and greed played the ugly role in settling the past; only for the few to benefit.

Now the American businessmen, such as those in banking and industry, will say that all they did was to benefit their company and promote jobs back in the U.S.A. The bankers will say that all they did was to protect the bank's investors and depositors. The political leaders will say that the handing over of Okinawa, without reimbursement for improvements was to promote good will towards Japan. Former President Nixon will say that all he did was as he was told by Former President Eisenhower. All will have an excuse of some sort. But the bottom line is why did Former President Eisenhower, and former President Nixon, sign over U.S. funds to personal political nationalists in Japan. The only assumption one can make is that someone, or ones, made out financially like a bandit. All at the expense of the taxpayers of the United States of America, knowing full well that they would never be discovered. Their protection was the Minister of Finance and the political business leaders of Japan.

The reason for the delay, or crack, is the mentality of the large corporations in the U.S. and Japan. Greed has taken over (not that it ever left), and now has become more obvious as American Corporations become more global and adjust to the excesses of the last twenty years. The Trust could utilize these Securities through another country and still maintain its objectives. The only real loser would be the U.S. taxpayer. A letter was sent, by Express Mail, to President bush, prior to the 1992 election, informing him of the Securities. And over the last three years, notification was made to the top agencies in the U.S. Government as well, stating the Trust's ability to help resolve the four trillion dollar foreign debt problem. No one responded in those last three years including President Bush

The Trust and the Chairman always are looking ahead, long range, ten to fifteen years, as to the unification of Europe and Russia as to their ability to survive, and the United States, as to the time it will take to get back on a narrow track of conservatism and correct what has happened over the past thirty years. Asia and more specifically, Japan, as they relate to North America.

The Chairman always stated that Europe will not unite into one, quickly, because of the different cultures, hatreds between countries, and the distrust of others. It will take two to three generations to resolve these differences.

Asia is safe because of its ability to produce, its disciplined workers and its natural resources. Asia needs the United States market to sell – export. As an example is Japan, who has two goals: one expansion, and two export to survive. The accomplish this is the requirement for imports, raw material from Asia and United States of America.

The United States needs discipline. It is a safe place to operate from but it has many problems. The goal of the Trust is to purchase goods for export, which in turn creates jobs and taxes for the U.S.A. One of the many problems for the Trust in dealing with the United States is the brokerage system, as well as the legal system. Brokers, for the most part, do not contribute to the economy, only for themselves. Lawyers in the United States take over the deals and dictate the terms of contracts. In Europe, lawyers are told what to do, period. Everywhere you turn, there is a broker; IBM, digital, ATT, etc. They have all turned to the brokerage system, not sales; in this way employees work on a billable time basis for their pay. A way to generate money and not totally to sell equipment.

The Chairman asked me not to deal with any middlemen or women, or brokers at any level. Of course you can not buy insurance without an agent. So I had to adjust my thinking to go directly for information, prices, and bids. This method is harder and makes you think and work additional time to figure out where to obtain the contracts. After many, many months of adjusting, it is now very easy to make one or two calls to deal directly without the middlemen or brokers, which has become second nature to me now. When I reflect back, I was inexperienced, unprofessional, and did not follow through with research in every small aspect of any project prior to my retooling.

LAW OFFICES

NISHIMURA & SANADA

YOSHIRO NISHIMURA   MASAHITO AMANO
RIHIRO SANADA   ANITOSHI NAKAMURA
JITCHIKO AIBA   SHINICHI TAKAHASHI
ATSURO TANAKA   ATSUO DOHKE
MASAHIRO SHIMOJO   HIROYUKI SHIMIZU
AKIRA KOSUGI   ATSUSHI NAITO
EIZO MATSUO   HIROYUKI TEZUKA
MASARU ONO   MASAHIRO UENO
EIICHI KASHIHARA   MITSUKO MIYAGAWA
EMIKO KASAHARA   MASAKAZU MAKURA
KOICHI KUSANO   HIROTO TERASHIMA
TOMOHITO TOHYAMA   SHINTO TERAMOTO
TAKASHI YONEDA   OSAMU SHIHARA
SATOSHI OGISHI   KOZO KAWAI
HITOMI OSHIKIRI   MITSUHIRO KAMIYA
HIDEAKI OZAWA   TOSHIHIRO MAEDA
AKIMITSU KAMORI   TOSHINO OSHIMA
KATSU SENGOKU
RYOSUKE ITO
TAKANOBU TAKEHARA   HIDETOSHI ASAKURA *
KEN KAWABATA   TSUNEMASA TERAI *
SACHIO WATANABE   * CURRENTLY ON LEAVE

4TH FLOOR
KASUMIGASEKI BUILDING
2-5, KASUMIGASEKI 3-CHOME
CHIYODA-KU, TOKYO 100
JAPAN

OF COUNSEL
MASATOMI KOMATSU
TAKAHISA SUGANO

TELEPHONE: (03) 593-3911
TELEX: J27691 JURISTS
CABLE: JURISTS TOKYO
TELECOPIER (03) 508-8289
(03) 591-4837
(03) 593-3916
(03) 593-3909

April 25, 1989

Dr. ▓▓▓▓▓▓▓▓▓▓
Chairman
▓▓▓▓▓▓▓▓▓▓▓▓▓▓▓▓▓▓▓▓▓▓

Dear Dr. ▓▓▓▓▓:

This is to report to you the actions we have taken
pursuant to your request.

First, we called on April 24, 1989 Ms. Uchida of U.S.
Embassy in Tokyo at 03-224-5645, and obtained from her the
following telephone numbers at the U.S. State Department:

    202-634-4000
    202-647-2912   Secretary to Mr. William Breer

    202-647-2913   Direct number to Mr. William Breer,
                    Director, Office of Japanese
                    Affairs, East Asia and Pacific
                    Affairs.

Then, we called Mr. William Breer at 202-647-2912 at
10:00 p.m. April 24, 1989 (Tokyo time), and he confirmed with
us the following points:

1.   At the request of Mr. Olson of Complex Industries
      Holdings Ltd. ("CIH"), Mr. Breer was expecting our
      call.

2.   Mr. Breer had a meeting with Mr. Olson and he
      believes he has received from Mr. Olson the
      following letters:

121

A. Letter, dated January 23, 1989

addressed to the:

Secretary of Treasury, Nicholas P. Brady

signed by Mr. Martin Olson, on behalf of
Dr. ██████ Chairman, outlining the entire
program concerning the joint ventures with
Japanese companies, the effect concerning the
trade deficit in conjunction with Japan and
the effect to the U.S. budget deficit.

B. Letter, dated January 24, 1989, No. 92315/424

addressed to:

Secretary Brady, signed by Dr. Mihaly

confirming the explanation made by Mr. Olson,
outlining the international political global
effect of CIH's project.

C. Letter, dated January 25, 1989

addressed to:

Treasury Department, to Meg Lundsager

containing various legal aspects, inside of
U.S.A.

D. Letter, dated February 1, 1989

addressed to:

Department of Commerce, Secretary of
Commerce, Robert Mosbacher

outlining the trade relating mechanism.

E. Letter, dated February 1, 1989

addressed to:

Chief of Staff Governor Sununu

thanking him for all of his arrangements.

- 3 -

    We trust the foregoing is responsive to your request.
If you need any further assistance, please call.

                              Very truly yours,

                              [signature]
                          for Masahiro Shimojo

MS:ao

(訳　文)

Complex Industries Holdings Ltd.

会長 Sandor Nihaly 殿

親愛なる ■■■■■■ 殿

　この手紙は、貴殿の依頼で我々が行ったことの内容を貴殿に伝えるものです。

　第1に、我々は、1989年4月24日、03-224-5645番に電話し、東京にある米国大使館の内田女史と話し、彼女から米国国務省の以下の電話番号を教えられました。

　　　202-634-4000
　　　202-647-2912　　William Breer 氏の秘書
　　　202-647-2913　　East Asia and Pacific Affairs 及び Japanese
　　　　　　　　　　　　Affairs 部の課長 William Breer 氏の直通番号

　次に我々は、1989年4月24日午後10時(東京時間)に202-647-2912番に電話し、William Breer 氏と話しました。そこで彼は、我々に対し以下のことを確認しました。

1　■■■■■■■■■■■■ Ltd.(「CIH」)の Olson 氏の依頼で Breer 氏は、我々の電話を待っていた。

2　Breer 氏は Olson 氏と会談したことがあり、Olson 氏から以下の手紙を受取ったと思う。

　　(イ)　1989年1月23日付の手紙
　　　　　　で
　　　　　財務省長官 Nicholas P. Brady
　　　　　宛の ■■■■■■ 氏の代理人 Martin Olson 氏により署名されたもの。これには日本企業との合弁事業に関する全計画、日本との貿易不均衡及び米国の財政赤字に対する影響の概要が記載されていた。

　　(ロ)　1989年1月24日付手紙(92315/424)
　　　　　　で
　　　　　Nihaly 氏が署名し Brady 長官
　　　　　に宛たもの。これは、Olson 氏の説明を確認するもので、またCIHの計画が国際政治に与える影響の概要が記されていた。

(ハ)　<u>1989年1月25日付の手紙</u>

　　　　　　で

　<u>財務省の Meg Lundsager</u>

　宛のもの。これには米国内での各種法的側面についての記載があった。

(ニ)　<u>1989年2月1日付の手紙</u>

　　　　　　で

　<u>商務省長官 Robert Mosbacher</u>

　宛のもの。これには通商関連のメカニズムについて記載されていた。

(ホ)　<u>1989年2月1日付手紙</u>

　　　　　　で

　Cheif of Staff Governor である Sununu

　宛のもの。これは彼が行った手配について謝意を述べるものであった。

　我々は、以上が貴殿の依頼を満たすものと信じています。更に何かお手伝いすることが
あればお電話下さい。

　　　　　　　　　　　　　　　　　　　　　　　　　　　　　　敬具

　　　　　　　　　　　　　　　　　　弁護士 下　綜　正　尚

以上正訳しました。

弁護士　高　橋　真

CHAPTER SEVEN

Conclusion of the Japanese Notes

This is a summary of the Japanese notes:

B UT WAIT, I THOUGHT this was over, but no. The Doctor revised and worked on a new plan to use the Japanese notes, about which I did not know, until I found an October 15, 2001 memo, which was written just before his passing.

The total of the Japanese notes was 600 billion U.S. dollars, plus interest, to cover the rebuilding of Japan after World War II, and to be repaid to the U.S. Government. Now it has been laundered, so that the notes are only good if the Japanese Government says yes, which means that they will never be paid by the Japanese Government. This was arranged by their attorney in the U.S.A., Richard Nixon.

Japan and the United States are totally two different cultures with the same basic problem of control and greed, which is the common thread throughout the world. Japan with its ancient culture and its basis to have a closed society, verses the young American culture and its basis to have an open society. Japan controls its society through secret societies, the "Zaibatsu," and the discipline of the Japanese People. The United States controls its society through its political leaders, banking and industrial leaders, and the limited knowledge allowed to be exposed to their society. The average United States citizen does not have any interest in global topics, as we have had no wars since the Civil War, and have had it our way since 1950's. The Japanese have had it well only since the 1950's and have had only limited growth in the country at the expense of its hard working citizens. The Japanese CD's, which total about 600 million dollars, plus interest, is equal to approximately 20% of the US deficit. The American politicians are trying to dance around the problems the U.S. faces.

The history of these Japanese CD securities should be reviewed as they relate to both cultures and the control and greed of its political system, banking and industrial leaders:

1. General Douglas MacArthur announced in 1945 no reparation with U.S. to provide assistance in the rebuilding of Japan.
2. The involvement of certain U.S. politicians, U.S. Banking Chairmen and U.S. major corporations to protect their investments and to profit in the future.
3. President Eisenhower in 1960 could have demanded repayment of U.S. aid, which enabled not only reparations from Japan industries but also U.S. aid in the form of loans and notes. Of course, none of this was done.
4. Nixon, in April 1964, started to visit Japan annually and represented Japan's concerns.
5. In 1972, Nixon signed over Okinawa to the Japanese government with all of its infrastructure fully repaired and completed, free of any charge by the US Government.
6. Nixon, at the same time in 1972, while Okinawa was signed over by President Decree by President Eisenhower, also signed over all the U.S. aid and reparations due to the U.S. to the political nationalists of Japan.
7. President Gerald Ford gave Richard Nixon a pardon from January 20, 1969, thru August 9, 1974. This was for the Watergate Affair, and other deeds such as the Japanese notes.

The last chain of events triggered the personal wealth of many business and political leaders of Japan, who had already misused these funds, as well as, undoubtedly, a few American politicians. The past subject has been well known to the U.S.A. by some of the political leaders, major law offices, and U.S. Government agencies. It was, and still is, a very well kept secret from the U.S. citizens as well as the average Japanese citizen. As of now, the Japanese people and the American people believe that all the past Japanese reparations were handled properly, and settled in the proper legal way. Little does the U.S. and Japanese citizen know that control and greed played the ugly role in settling the past; only for a few to benefit.

In only a few instances would the subject of the notes ever again come to the forefront. Once was when a woman, operating in Japan on behalf of the Russian KGB, had been sent there to see if the notes actually did exist and, if so, to find out where they were being kept. As a part of her action, and armed with the limited information she possessed, she was to become romantically involved with an officer at the bank that was believed to hold these securities. She was successful in determining that the notes were, in fact, in evidence at the bank as she was one of a very few people to witness their existence in these later years. She followed her instructions from the KGB to the letter.

Before long she gained the confidence of the bank officer and became involved in a passionately heated liaison. Discovering that the bank officer with whom she was having an affair suffered from diabetes and required daily inoculations of insulin, she offered her assistance in giving him his required injections. In time she was able to introduce a poison into his viles of insulin. She altered the doses of the medicine so that when it was injected, the effects resulted in his gradually dying. Upon his death, she managed to abscond with a portion of the notes and disappeared. Instead of returning to Russia, she went into hiding. No one ever knew what happened to her or to the missing notes. The KGB sent operatives looking to find her but if she was ever found that information did not come to light. The chances are that if she was located, she never survived to see the next day.

The second instance when the notes came to the forefront happened when a friend of the Chairman, Norbert Schlei, an attorney who was an assistant U.S. Attorney General under President John Kennedy, was indicted by the United States Secret Service for counterfeiting and for trying to sell Japanese bonds with a face value of 2.2 billion dollars to a Tampa, Florida bank. These were some of the MacArthur Fund Japanese notes. The case against Schlei took five years and were dismissed by the U.S. attorney and the judge at the request of the federal prosecutor.

A similar case involving fifty billion dollars in Japanese notes was also dismissed by the court with no explanation. Although the Secret Service officials hailed this case as the larges in history, the Japanese government said this was the work of skilled forgers. No one from either side wanted to admit the existence of these funds so it was better to keep the issue buried by whatever means possible – i.e. both cases were dismissed by the court for lack of evidence or political pressure, and charges of forgery. In every instance, all bases had to be covered. This was true when notes surfaced in Nevada, New York, and South Carolina. Where they came from or how they emerged is a subject for conjecture. No one seemed to know and the less t hat was known, the better. The Japanese government had always denied the existence of the MacArthur notes which, as mentioned before, cannot be sold, traded or used as collateral without their permission.

The only other time the notes came into play was as a result of my disdain for what the leaders of our country tried to do to protect their own selfish interests, the ones who could not have given a damn as to what happened to the rest of the country. Had I not been the chosen courier for Dr. Mihaly and the Swiss Trust, I might never have known about this secret fund. Being a businessman with a sense of ethics and a patriotic dedication to the United States, I could not turn a blind eye to this financial rape that was perpetrated upon America. Had I not been so uncompromising in my morality, I suppose I could have adopted the same lines of excuses many in our country I would use in doing business. The American businessman, such as those involved in industry, will say when it comes to the subject of having negotiated with Japan that all of what they did was to benefit their companies and promote jobs back in the States. The bankers will say that all they did was to protect their investors and depositors. The political leaders will say that the handing over of Okinawa, without reimbursement for improvements, was to promote goodwill towards Japan. Former President Nixon will say he did what he did because he was told to by former President Eisenhower. All good-sounding reasons that are nothing more than excuses. The only assumption one can make is that someone or ones made out financially like a bandit knowing full well that they would never be discovered and all at the expense of the American taxpayer who would have no knowledge of what took place. All the excuse-givers would be protected by the Minister of Finance and the political leaders in Japan.

I could not let this go. The value of the CD's on today's market, including interest, would be over a trillion dollars, a staggering amount our government is willing to throw away. Because of the enormity of the sum and because the exposure of this scandal would be so embarrassing to our government, the inner circle of leaders is willing to do whatever it takes to eliminate anyone who might bring the facts of the MacArthur

Funds to light. It is better left among the non-existent. To emphasize their fervor in maintaining this secret, I was subjected to pressure from the U.S. Secret Service and my family threatened to the point of never having lived.

It is frightening to think that our government is so enormous that a trillion dollars can be made to vanish with no accounting for its ever being. Or that our government is so powerful that it can annihilate anyone or any group of people who can expose it for the wrongdoing of those few who are in control. Keep in mind that the officials in the United States are well aware of the CD's and their representing the long overdue payment for the reparation of Japan. They are also aware about the Trust's efforts regarding using the CD's to start to repay the United States for the Second World War. The object of the Trust program was for the benefit of both countries by making these CD's collectible. Both parties were originators – Japan issuing the CD's, and the United States supplying the funds. Up to this point it seemed to me that the only people losing out were the American taxpayers. I was amazed how two governments were able to hide this information for so many years: four-plus decades of intrigue, corruption, and profit for just a select few.

The following collateral memo was made by Dr. Mihaly on October 15, 2001, just two months before his death. The Doctor was trying to restart the use of the Japanese notes so as to build his medical university and help the U.S. to receive some of their money lent to Japan in 1952 for the rebuilding of Japan. Now those 1952 agreements were revised in 1959-60 by Vice-President Richard Nixon so that Japan would never have to repay their debt to the U.S.A.

QUALITY OF COLLATERAL.
(10-15-2001)

1015-QUALITY

TORONTO COMPANY, owned by DR. SANDOR MIHALY, as majority will have the arrangement to obtain the permit from the US FEDERAL RESERVE BANK to use the CERTIFICATES OF REDEMPTION AS COLLATERAL, issued in Japanese yen.

Above arrangement is to be in accordance with the

SECRETE PROTOCOL
TO THE MUTUAL SECURITY TREATY
BETWEEN U.S. AND JAPAN,
SIGNED ORIGINALLY IN 1952,
REVISED IN 1959-60,
AFTER NEGOTIATION BETWEEN
VICE PRESIDENT NIXON
AND
PRIME MINISTER KISHI.

It shall be noted, the true backing of these certificates is the Japanese Secrete fund.
The fund has staggering amount of assets; mostly gold but many other types of assets as well, so that THE CERTIFICATES, UNDER CONTROL OF TORONTO COMPANY, REALLY

MUCH MORE SECURE THAN
ORDINARY JAPANESE GOVERNMENT OBLIGATIONS.

Sincerely:

DR. SANDOR MIHALY

CHAPTER EIGHT

Gold & Projects

THIS IS A REPORT, which lightly touches on the issues of the Doctor's medical problems, and how he handled them as he maintained his grip on the Trust business for which he was responsible.

Dr. Mihaly suffered from Crohn's Disease, as well as a number of other ailments. His discomfort was, to him, a nuisance, but he would not allow it to interfere with the work he felt needed to be accomplished. He was a computer nut, so he moved in all his computers to the hospital. He had to have all the latest technology. He had to have that because he had agents operating all over the world, in every country, reporting to him every day.

Anything in the world that was political was of interest to him. That included, especially, anything having to do with the movement of money or precious metals or anything in the medical field. He would give these agents tasks, i.e. research somebody, their background, or their involvements in whatever projects piqued his interest. I was asked to be there every day to discuss the progress being made. In fact, when I was a currier, transporting money to Japan – 18 billion dollars of notes from the MacArthur Fund – I didn't know that I was being followed by one of his agents. He had me followed so that he could be sure that I did exactly what he wanted me to do without any deviation. He was constantly in touch with Switzerland, his prime location, as well as all of his agents. Money talks – that is why there was no question about him having all of his computer equipment in his hospital room. I had to go in every day and we would have a session, discuss whatever topic related to gold, petroleum, petro-chemical, hydro-electrics, satellite systems, everything. My job was to do all the talking to everyone concerned with his interests around the world.

While the Doctor was in the hospital he asked me to research the moving of gold bullion, and also the manufacturing of vaccines. He also wanted me to continue with the research that I originally worked on regarding the Irish Satellite system that I mentioned earlier. This was for all types of communications throughout the world. And it became a heavy, money-making, pet project for the Hughes Company.

Howard Hughes wanted the Trust to finance this Irish Satellite System, which had a very broad base and that would involve a great deal of money. And the Doctor said that until Martin understands all the satellite system, we can't give you a yes or no. "As a matter of fact," he told Howard Hughes, "we can't do anything until Martin knows everything about you as well, or we can't touch it." That was because I was Dr. Mihaly's business secretary and I was entrusted with knowing every detail about the Doctor's anticipated projects. After talking with Howard Hughes and all his staff about the Doctor and the Trust, I get a fax from them saying that everything I told them about the Trust was true because Hughes' intelligence people did their own investigation of the Trust in Switzerland and they found out that it is real and they do have the money and the power to undertake anything the Doctor decides.

We were going to pay for its launching and its ground control. It involved three or four of these radio satellite devices to go into orbit. And we had it down to the point where I told the Doctor this looks good, it's a go, if you're ready we should do it. And it came down to the wire and suddenly, at the last minute, the Doctor reneged on it because he was afraid he might lost the Trust Fund where billions were involved.

It is fascinating when one considers the wide spread of the many types of projects, which the Doctor wanted to investigate. There was never a dull moment working for the Doctor.

So, the Doctor is in the hospital, St. Mary's Hospital, in West Palm Beach, Florida, waiting to be operated on, and he has his computers and phone lines set up in his room, as he is working daily on his numerous projects; and all with hospital approval.

Dr. Sandor Mihaly was a true scientist. His mind was trained, as a scientist, to prove everything, and not to accept anything at face value. Dr. Mihaly, as Chairman of the Silent Trust, was always afraid to make a mistake and risk any loss of Trust assets. Therefore, it was difficult for the Doctor to proceed easily with any major projects.

The difference in men is not in the opportunities that come to them, but in their use of these opportunities. Many people who fail to make much of their opportunities, charge their failure to start any project with excuses that the project has too many flaws and risks.

All the projects, except a hospital built by the Trust for Kuwait, which is a depositor of the Trust, presented to the Doctor were not in the scientific field of medicine, but in projects for the Silent Trust. Now this meant risk, so no projects were actually started. What a waste. So many hospitals, clinics, housing, petrochemical plants, and many other projects could have been built and operated to serve mankind but those opportunities were passed by, never to come again in the Doctor's life.

"God broke our years to hours and days, that hour by hour and day to day, just going on a little way, we might be able all along to keep quite strong. Should all the weight of life be laid across our shoulder, and the future, ripe with woe and struggle, meet us face to face at just one place. We could not go, our feet would stop; and so God lays a little on us every day, and never, I believe, on all the way will burdens bear so deep, or pathways lie so threatening and so steep, but we can go, if by God's power we only bear the burden of the hour." Miller

Living, thus, we shall make each hour radiant with the radiancy of duty. Work done, and radiant hours, will make radiant years. But the missing of privileges and the neglecting of duties will leave days and years marred and blemished. We must catch the sacred meaning of our opportunities if we would live up to our best.

With all that the Chairman had for upcoming projects, my wife and I decided that it would be better if we moved back to Florida to work with him. He was scheduled to return from California later during 1989. The reason my wife and I made our decision to go there before him was because my wife was diagnosed with cancer and surgery was imminent. This started a long process of treatments down a rocky road for which I again needed iron shoes.

Shortly after the return of the Chairman, he came down with salmonella and *e coli* and he demanded that I be with him every day that he was in the hospital. I was amazed to see how the hospital personnel catered to him. They set up computers and equipment in his room, not only to monitor his progress but to allow him to continue to conduct his business from his bedside. He had hook-ups to Switzerland and everywhere else that he did business. In truth, he took over the entire hospital. So, now I am doing research for him while caring for my wife at the same time. It is unreal how controlling and demanding a person the Chairman is. Here I am, running between St. Mary's Hospital in West Palm Beach where he was recuperating, and my home where my wife is dying.

I think what astonished me the most was the fact that, in the hospital, he directed the surgery on himself; he gave the doctors instructions on what they were to do for him. They were to cut out a large portion of his lower bowel. This man was so intelligent that he had a hard time communicating with anybody. The main reason he had me with him was just for that purpose. I was his liaison.

Once he recovered, it would again be business as usual. I found myself still at his beck and call. Although he was back on his feet he continued to want me to carry out his requests, including courier service to all parts of the world.

The Chairman asked me to do some research into moving gold bullion from vaults in Jakarta, Indonesia to the Zurich, Switzerland Airport, where the government has vaults on the premises.

I asked him where the gold bullion, made up of gold bars, came from and he told me that just before the United States, through MacArthur, took over Japan, the gold bars were buried under water. In time, they were moved to Jakarta. They were owned by the government and certain officials gave them over to the Swiss Trust for safe keeping. I was never told what arrangements or exchange was made between the officials and the Trust.

The Chairman asked me to include in my research, studies and costs for moving the gold also to New York and to West Palm Beach as well as to France and to Zurich, Switzerland. During the course of these studies, I further investigated gold ore refining and recovery, and was surprised to find that 5000 tons of ore can be mined per day, and that for every ton of ore, only a minute number of ounces of pure gold can be realized per ton.

I never did find out whatever was done with the gold. As I said before, many of the Chairman's projects were either not fulfilled or, if they were, they were done without my knowledge. Everything the Swiss do is with great secrecy so, if the gold was moved, left in the vaults, or if the Trust transferred ownership, I had no idea. I was told, however, that the gold was removed from Japan so that the U.S. could not have access to it. I am sure that certain Japanese higher-ups have managed to take it for their own personal use.

At a later date, the Chairman wanted me to do some research into the manufacturing and production of pharmaceuticals. With his having successfully patented more than 75 substances for the medical community, this was a natural evolution. His goal was to search and then manufacture his discoveries. In the process of doing this, he became involved with the Federal Drug Administration and their requirements for clinical trials. Everything he proposed was to be done in concert with the medical university in Palm Beach, Florida and also with the one in Switzerland. He further wanted to incorporate India in these medical projects.

I spent months doing the research of methods, operation, and the cost on vaccine manufacturing. I contacted such companies as Doerfer Engineering out of Orlando, Florida. They designed and implemented the medical facilities for Disney World and other large medical centers. I engaged in a study in which there was a vaccine process that can produce 1000 viles per minute, and even more with a second assembly line. The problem was always with the production of the live virus and maintaining stability of the virus as well as determining how long it will last.

In completing my research, I suggested the use of a robotic system to facilitate laboratory production. In the areas of food processing, it would make sense to utilize the flash-freezing method based upon the discovery made by the Doctor in Austria after World War II. This process would have been ideal in preserving the tissues used for vaccine production as well.

COPY

Certificate of the Incorporation of a Company

No. 187 of 1990

STATE OF GRENADA.

I hereby Certify that

" EUROINVEST INTERNATIONAL BANK

AND TRUST LIMITED "

is this day incorporated under "The Companies Ordinance, 1926," (No 18 of 1926) and that the Company is limited.

Given under my hand at Saint George's this 6th day of November, one thousand nine hundred and ninety.

CERTIFIED A TRUE COPY

REGISTRAR

S. Belfon

Sandra Belfon
Acting Registrar of Companies.

Registration Fees $ 240.00

Stamp Duty $ 15.00

Form of Original Certificate of Incorporation.

Certificate received by

Date 11/6 - 90

88a

UNION BANK OF SWITZERLAND

Bank of Commercial Trusty
No. 6008979922 / B / 16 / 1969

International F.C.D Bank, 56400229886 / V / 34241 / December / 12 / B Swiss F.O
995646611 / Switzerland F.O 07757750 / Zurriche C.D 231 / Geneva F.O 342188671 /
Legalized C.D.O 99956166 / Cioriel Eioersrische 40/B/600078688/Commercial Bank.
Based on the decision International Certificate D.C Calculation Invest F.L.P
Deposit Union Bank of Switzerland, 54388676776 / N.L.3 97 / B.
Legalized C.L.M Deposit C.H No. 677564663300 / B / 1422122 / B.L.N

    Governor C.L.N Union Bank of Switzerland
       No. 67755400897991.C.G. 1969
    Finance of Central Ministry
    Government B.L.J No. 66650089799 / V.H / 1969
    President of Commisaries C.L.N Bank
       No. 677453551007.C.L.N 1969
    Secretary of Bullion International Department
       No. 600078488488 / B.H / 341 / 1969

C.L.B Deposit Holder :

       B.M.C, 5430089799 R.I 00001 C. 0045355
       T.L.M 00675771105646644.G.L.B 64 / B / 978688
       L.M.D 231886757750086 / V.L / 2319976 / 00045.

C.L.N Deposit	C.L.N Time Year	Call Max	C.H.P Deposit
Metal F. 7756	July, 1949	Invest	F.C 23./F/089
Bank C.T	V.H Cols Transaction	B.j Platinum	....
Metal C.J 7564	Deposit Collateral	Platinum F.C	G.L.N 977/V/3
Officel C.D/67/U	....	....	....
Metal F.C 5342	Deposit Invest	Platinum T.C	....
Bank Off	C.H 756466.B.	....	....
Metal C.L.J	Transaction f	....	....
Bank C.G	....	....	....
Gold C.L Metal	....	....	....
Collateral C.LM / BG	....	....	....
Collateral Invest	....	Transaction	....
Obligation C.L.N	....	Transaction	C.L.N 755454/C
Obligation F.L.P	....	Deposit C.L.S	....
Obligation F. Collat	....	Deposit F.L.P	....
Collateral G.L.D	....	T.L. 543/B/54	....
Collateral D.L.P	....	Deposit C.K	....
Collateral F.O.P	T.M.H 7554/C/8777	....	B.L.N 786/L/B

    Special Date C.L.N Holder Transaction
    F.C.L Union International Bank

C.L.N Date Bank 655455 /1B / No. 5000078688. 1969

C.L.N Metal Deposit	Collateral Max. Time Year	F.L.J Bank
Platinum V.L.N 76566	Collateral Invest 1959	V.L.N 999 / C / 564
Platinum D.V. 4535100	Collateral Invest 1969	T.L.P 0776 / V / 43
Platinum C.L.N 45350	Collateral Invest 1969	C.L.N 7564 / L / 341
Platinum D.C.L 342886	Collateral Invest 1970	G.L.P 543992 / L / 4
Platinum F.L.P 453551	Collateral Invest 1974	
Platinum F.L.P 3424	Collateral Invest 1976	
Platinum F.L.P 6665009	Collateral Invest 1985	
Platinum C.H 86757	Collateral Invest 1989	
Platinum R.L.M 756466	Collateral Invest 1990	G.L.M 97862 / B
Platinum C.L.N 4535	Collateral Deposit 1991	G.L.P 45355 / N
Platinum D.L.P 43233	Collateral Transaction 1994	G.L.P 43 L / M
Platinum S.V 75	Collateral Transaction 1997	B.J.L 977677 / L
Platinum C.G 867	Collateral Transaction 1999	G.L.N 86 / B.L
Platinum D.L.P 86757	Collateral Transaction 2005	G.L.P 8675 / L
Gold C.L.N Transaction	Collateral Transaction 1967	V.L.M 342442 / L
Gold C.L.N Transaction	Collateral Transaction 1978	H.L.P 4323397
Gold V.L.M Transaction	Collateral Transaction 1990	B.L.M 54388
Gold G.L.P Transaction	Collateral Transaction 2007	B.L 65499 / M / 08
Obligation Transaction	Collateral Transaction 1950	V.L 543443 / L /D
Obligation Transaction	Collateral Transaction 2002	G.L.N 756466.L.

54329786886.L.N.J 0089799

C.L.N New Holder C1L.N 8675775/N/5640089799

Time, Year ....

Deposit C.L.N Transaction ....

Metal B.L.J .... Kgs.

Trust C.L.N ....

Name B.H Mr. ....

Mrs. ....

Nationality ....

Code ....

47098. L.A.3182
ASSAY SUISSE MERCIE
SUISSE
INCHRISSEY 27 GENEVA

President of Commissaries
Union Bank of Switzerland
C.L.N 8665/M/088788/23133

Bangko Sentral ng Pilipinas
(CENTRAL BANK OF THE PHILIPPINES)
East Avenue, Quezon City

MINT & GOLD REFINERY

DELIVERY RECEIPT

D R N⁰ 11381

000007

REFERENCE:

DO No: _____

DATE: December 13, 1983

Delivered to __TOMAS RODRIGUEZ, Tanaw Security Services, INC._ (ex-Gold Refinery)
the following: in behalf of JOHNSON MATTHEY COMMODITIES, LONDON

PARTICULARS	WEIGHT (GROSS)	ASSAY		CONTENTS (OZ. TR.)	
		GOLD	SILVER	GOLD	SILVER
1. EKF Residue 45 Drums	7,781.6			2,971.652	39,553.417
2. Minus 40 Mesh Residue					
26 Drums	7,250.9			527.841	5,555.572
-x-x-x-x-x-x-x-x-x-x-x-x-x Nothing follows x-x-x-x-x-x-x-x-x-x-x-x-x					

Contained in:

Released For Delivery
NOTE:

Processed and Packed By

_____
Technical Assistant

Chief, Stock Count Division

Received the above-mentioned delivery
in good order and condition:

_____
TOMAS RODRIGUEZ
Representative
Date: December 13, 1983
Tanaw Security Services, Inc.

Witnessed By:

_____
Representative — Office of the
the Operations Division, FED

EDUARDO O. ESTRADA Auditor
Treasury Office of the
Director, FED

Representative — Security & Transport
Department, CBP

Bangko Sentral ng Pilipinas
(CENTRAL BANK OF THE PHILIPPINES)
East Avenue, Quezon City

MINT & GOLD REFINERY

DELIVERY RECEIPT DR Nº 141

REFERENCE:

DO No. 118

DATE: January 19, 1984

Delivered to TREASURY, CBP thru Mr. EUGENE TY, Technical Assistant (ex-Gold Refinery)
the following:

PARTICULARS	WEIGHT (OZ. TR.)	ASSAY		CONTENTS (OZ. TR.)	
		GOLD	SILVER	GOLD	SILVER
ONE HUNDRED ELEVEN (111)					
GOOD DELIVERY BARS					
Nos. A 03376 to A 03486	43,216.225	99.56	—	43,027.456	—
	*Average Assay				

Contained in:

D. P. FLORES, JR.
Acting Director

Prepared and Packed By:

Chief, Stock Control Division

Received the above-mentioned delivery
in good order and condition:

EUGENE TY
Representative Treasury
Date: January 19, 1984

Witnessed By:

OSCAR TALEN VELASCODE
Representative — Office of the Deputy Director, MGR

BLAS S. SERRANA
Representative — Security & Transport
Department, CBP

Copy for the Cash Department, CBP

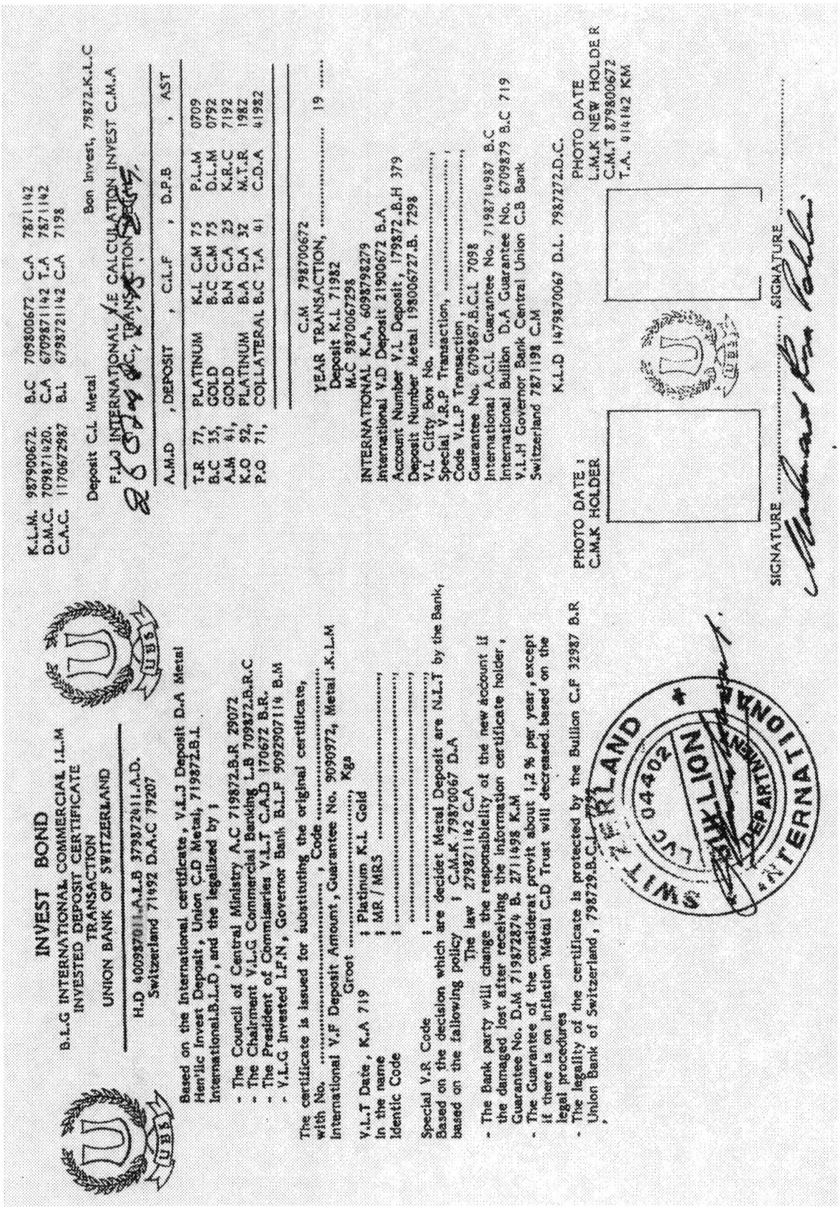

INVEST BOND
B.L.G INTERNATIONAL COMMERCIAL I.L.M
INVESTED DEPOSIT CERTIFICATE
TRANSACTION
UNION BANK OF SWITZERLAND

H.D 400987011.A.L.B 379872411.A.D.
Switzerland 71492 D.A.C 79207

Based on the International certificate, V.L.J Deposit D.A Metal Hen'lic Invest Deposit, Union C.D Metal, 719872.B.L International.B.L.D, and the legalized by ;

- The Council of Central Ministry A.C 719872.B.R 29072
- The Chairment V.L.G Commercial Banking L.B 709872.B.R.C
- The President of Commisaries V.L.T C.A.D 170672 B.R.
- V.L.G Invested I.F.N, Governor Bank B.L.F 9092907114 B.M

The certificate is issued for substituting the original certificate, with No. ...., Code ....
International V.F Deposit Amount, Guarantee No. 9090972, Metal .K.L.M
Groot ...., Kgs

V.L.T Date, K.A 719 ; Platinum K.L Gold
In the name ; MR / MRS ....;
Identic Code ; ....;
....;

Special V.R Code ; ....;
Based on the decision which are decidet Metal Deposit are N.L.T by the Bank, based on the fallowing policy ; C.M.K 79870067 D.A
The law 279871142 C.A

- The Bank party will change the responsibielity of the new account if the damaged lost after receiving the information certificate holder, Guarantee No. D.M 719872874 B. 2711498 K.M
- The Guarantee of the considerat provit about 1,2 % per year, except if there is on inflation Métal C.D Trust will decreased based on the legal procedures
- The legality of the certificate is protected by the Bullion C.F 32987 B.R Union Bank of Switzerland, 798729.B.C.L 7292

SWITZERLAND LVC 04402 BULLION DEPARTMENT INTERNATIONAL

K.L.M. 987900672. B.C 709800672 C.A 7871142
D.M.C. 709871420. C.A 6709871142 T.A 7871142
C.A.C. 1170672987 B.L 6798721142 C.A 7198

Deposit C.L Metal Bon Invest, 79872.K.L.C
F.L.J INTERNATIONAL V.E CALCULATION INVEST C.M.A
D.C, TRANSACTION METAL

A.M.D	, DEPOSIT	, C.L.F	, D.P.B	, AST
T.R 77,	PLATINUM	K.L C.M 75	P.L.M	0709
B.C 35,	GOLD	B.C C.M 75	D.L.M	0792
A.M 41,	GOLD	B.N C.A 25	K.R.C	7192
K.O 92,	PLATINUM	B.A D.A 32	M.T.R	1982
P.O 71,	COLLATERAL	B.C T.A 41	C.D.A	41982

C.M 798700672
YEAR TRANSACTION, ... 19 ......
Deposit K.L 71982
M.C 9870067298
INTERNATIONAL K.A, 6098798279
International V.D Deposit 21900672 B.A
Account Number V.L Deposit, 179872.B.H 379
Deposit Number Metal 198006727.B. 7298
V.L Cifty Box No. ....;
Special V.R.P Transaction, ...;
Code V.L.P Transaction, ...;
Guarantee No. 6709867.B.C.L 7098
International A.C.L Guarantee No. 7198714987 B.C
International Bullion D.A Guarantee No. 6709879 B.C 719
V.L.H Governor Bank Central Union C.B Bank
Switzerland 7871198 C.M

K.L.D 1479870067 D.L. 7987272.D.C.

PHOTO DATE :
C.M.K HOLDER

PHOTO DATE
L.M.K NEW HOLDER
C.M.T 879800672
T.A. 414142 KM

SIGNATURE ...., SIGNATURE ....

INVEST BOND

B.L.G INTERNATIONAL COMMERCIAL I.L.M
INVESTED DEPOSIT CERTIFICATE
TRANSACTION
UNION BANK OF SWITZERLAND

H.D 4009B701,I.A.L.B 37987241I.A.D.
Switzerland 71692 D.A.C 79207

Based on the International certificate , V.L.J Deposit D.A Metal
Hen'lic Invest Deposit , Union C.D Metal, 71987Z.B.I
International.B.L.D, and, the legalized by)

- The Council of Central Ministry A.C 71987Z.B.R 2907Z
- The Chairmen V.LG Commercial Banking L.B 70987Z.B.R.C
- The President of Commissaries V.L.T C.A.D 17067Z B.R.
- V.LG Invested LF.N , Governor Bank B.L.F 9092907114 B.M

The certificate is issued for substituting the original certificate,
with No. .... , Code ....
International V.F Deposit Amount , Guarantee No. 9090972, Metal .K.L.M
Groot .... Kgs

V.L.T Date, K.A 719   ; Platinum K.L Gold
In the name   ; MR / MR5
Identic Code   ;

Special V.R Code
Based on the decision which are decided Metal Deposit are N.L.T by the Bank,
based on the following policy : C.M.K 79870067 D.A
                 The law   27987114Z C.A

- The Bank party will change the responsibility of the new account if
  the damaged lost after receiving the information certificate holder ,
  Guarantee No. D.M 71987Z874 B. 271498 K.M
- The Guarantee of the considered provit about 1,2 % per year , except
  if there is an inflation Metal C.D Trust will decreased based on the
  legal procedures
- The legality of the certificate is protected by ....
  Union Bank of Switzerland , 79829.B.C.L.,

K.L.M. 9879006?2.
D.M.C. 70987114Z0.
C.A.C. 11706729B7

B.C 70980067Z CA 787114Z
CA 67098711142 T.A 7871142
B.I 67987211142 CA 7198

Deposit C.L Metal   Bon Invest, 7987Z.K.L.C
F.L.J INTERNATIONAL V.E CALCULATION INVEST C.M.A
V.C. TRANSACTION METAL

A.M.D	, DEPOSIT	, C.L.F	, D.P.B	, AST
T.R 77;	PLATINUM	K.I C.M 73	P.L.M	0709
B.C 35;	GOLD	B.C C.M 73	D.L.M	0792
A.M 41;	GOLD	B.N C.A 23	K.R.C	7192
K.O 92;	PLATINUM	B.A D.A 32	M.T.R	1982
P.O 71;	COLLATERAL B.C T.A 41		C.D.A	41982

C.M 79870067Z
YEAR TRANSACTION, ... , 19 ......
Deposit K.L 71982
M.C 987006729B

INTERNATIONAL K.A, 609879B279
International V.D Deposit 219006Z72 B.A
Account Number V.L Deposit, I7987Z.B.H 379
Deposit Number Metal 19800672Z.B. 729B
V.L City Box No. ....
Special V.L.P Transaction, ...;
Code V.L.P Transaction, ...;
Guarantee No. 6709B67.B.C.I 7098
International A.C.L Guarantee No. 71987149B7 B.C
International Bullion D.A Guarantee No. 6709B79 B.C 719
V.L.H Governor Bank Central Union C.B Bank
Switzerland 787119B C.M

K.L.D 147987006Z D.L. 7987Z72.D.C.

PHOTO DATE
C.M.K HOLDER

PHOTO DATE
L.M.X NEW HOLDER
C.M.T 87980067Z
T.A. 1/41142 KM

.... SIGNATURE

88g

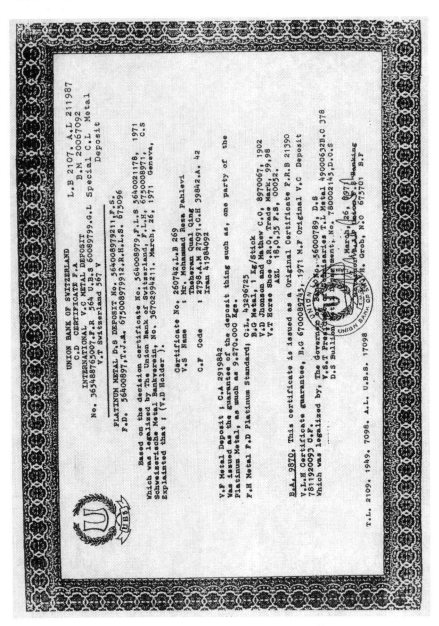

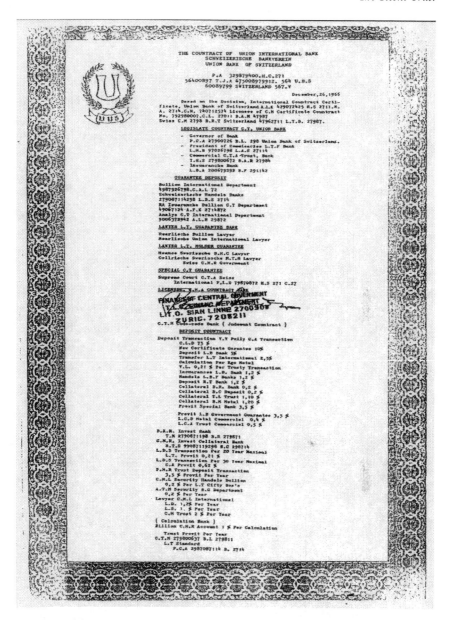

THE COUNTRACT OF UNION INTERNATIONAL BANK
SCHWEIZERISCHE BANKVEREIN
UNION BANK OF SWITZERLAND

P.A 329879400.H.C.271
56400897 T.J.A 675008979912. 564 U.B.S
60089799 SWITZERLAND 567.V

December,26,1966

Based on the Decision, International Countract Certi-
ficate, Union Bank of Switzerland,A.LX 429072425 H.S 2711.R.
A. 2714.C.M. 780712574 Licensee of C.H Certificate Countract
No. 792980007.C.L. 27011 D.A.M 47987
Swiss C.M 2798 B.R.T Switzerland 47962711 L.T.D. 27987.

LEGISLATE COUNTRACT C.T. UNION BANK

- Governor of Bank
  P.C.A 27900726 B.L. 298 Union Bank of Switzerland.
- President of Commission L.T.F Bank
  L.M.R 97026798 L.A.S 27114
- Commercial C.T.A Trust, Bank
  T.H.S 279800672 D.A.R 27984
- Insurances Bank
  L.R.A 200672929 R.F 291142

GUARANTEE DEPOSIT

Bullion International Department
4987926798.C.A.L 72
Schweizerische Handels Banks
279087114298 L.R.S 2714
RA Insuranches Bullion C.T Department
49067124 A.F.X 271 4872
Analys C.T International Department
7006372942 A.L.R 29872

LANTER L.T. GUARANTEE BANK

Heerlische Bullion Lawyer
Heerlische Union International Lawyer

LANTER L.T. HOLDER GUARANTEE

Heence Swerizsche B.H.C Lawyer
Collrische Swerizsche M.T.M Lawyer
Swiss C.H.R Government

SPECIAL C.T GUARANTEE

Supreme Court C.T.A Swiss
International F.X.D 79870872 N.S 271 C.27

LICENSEE: T.H.A COUNTRACT
FINANCE OF CENTRAL GOVERNMENT
T.L CURRANG DEPARTMENT
LIT.O. SIAN LINNE 27003DY
CURIC. 7208211
C.T.M Code-code Bank (Judesment Countract)

DEPOSIT COUNTRACT

Deposit Transaction V.T Fully C.A Transaction
C.L.D 73 %
New Certificate Garantee 10%
Deposit L.B Bank 5%
Transfer L.T International 2,5%
Calculation Per Age Metal
V.L. 0,21 % Per Trusty Transaction
Insurances L.B. Bank 1,2 %
Handels L.B.F Banks 1,2 %
Deposit R.T Bank 1,2 %
Collateral D.M. Bank 0,2 %
Collateral R.C Deposit 0,2 %
Collateral T.L Trust 1,10 %
Collateral B.M Metal 1,20 %
Provit Special Bank 3,3 %

Provit L.B Government Guarantee 3,5 %
L.C.D Metal Commercial 0,4 %
L.C.A Trust Commercial 0,5 %

B.R.M. Invest Bank
T.M 2790871198 B.R 279871
C.M.R. Invest Collateral Bank
R.T.S 99087119298 S.C 29871 4
L.D.S Transaction Per 20 Year Maximal
L.T. Provit 0,21 %
L.D.S Transaction Per 30 Year Maximal
C.A Provit 0,62 %
P.M.R Trust Deposit Transaction
3,5 % Provit Per Year
C.M.A Security Handels Bullion
0,2 % Per L.T City Bo's
A.T.M Security S.C Department
0,2 % Per Year
Lawyer C.M.L International
L.B. 1,2% Per Year
L.S. 1 % Per Year
C.M Trust 2 % Per Year

(Calculation Bank)
Billion C.H.R Account 1 % Per Calculation

Trust Provit Per Year
C.T.M 279800637 B.L 279811
L.T Standard
F.C.A 2987087114 B. 2714

145

CHAPTER NINE

The Medical University –
The Mission of Dr. Sandor Mihaly

THE DOCTOR HAD ME work on land for his mission to build a medical university in Florida that would serve the international medical community.

He told me that his mission in life was to establish a research hospital in order to continue looking for medicinal cures for diseases. He said, "Martin, that is also your mission. You've got to finish it." I worked on the design among all the other projects he had. The Doctor wanted to do this research hospital on the basis of this being in a central location so that any doctor or surgeon could call here, free, or get access to any of the latest procedures or technology. Also, the staff at the university could assist them by video of the latest techniques, free. He would be using the Trust money, because there was plenty of it, to build this and make it universally available for the benefit of all mankind. This hospital would be dedicated to research and teaching as well as practical health care. That was his dream and his mission. He wanted this to be built in West Palm Beach, Florida. Because he lived in Riviera Beach, Florida, he wanted the hospital to be reasonably close by so that he could oversee its building and operation. My concerns were that to build a hospital such as this in a place where the water table was high and the proximity to the ocean so close, that it would not be the best place to do this kind of construction. However, he was involved in so many immediate projects that this would not be looked at again until he had more time.

We first started with the MacArthur Group, which was located in Florida and in Hawaii. After lengthy discussions, the location was moved to the outskirts of Palm Beach, Florida on 600 acres of land. The following is an outline of the project. The Doctor had a contract prepared for signing of the 600 acres in June of 2000, but it did not close.

The Proposed Health Care Research and Practical Operation facility

Without criticizing the present United States of America Healthcare System, one may analyze its characteristics for the purpose to deduce what is the more efficient structure of a hospital or what we will call 'clinic,' the usual European terminology for institutions under the umbrella of a medical university and, in this case, a medical school.

The major part of the American hospital system is, in essence, an investment business, whereby the patients care stays in a secondary place behind investment strategies. The doctors are under control of the business establishment, therefore they are not independent intellectual forces.

The American Universities, their hospitals mostly financed by government sources, or are corporations for non-profit having not enough financial strength, with respect to the above mentioned profit-oriented hospitals, may consequently be influenced by the intellectual forces who even have certain independency, however that independency is truncated by the scarcity of financial tools.

World-wide known famous American Hospitals and Medical Schools are the driving forces of the advancement of the medical sciences, named Health Sciences, however the patients care is subordinated to financial barriers, for which the intellectual scientific staff is not to be blamed.

Of course, this reasoning does not discount the lead position of the American scientific and practical clinical activities, but the above referred discrepancies can be eliminated only by such kind of organization, which has absolute independency from government or public funds-related financial sources.

There is another consideration, which regards the current existing so-called information crisis; it means that in the whole world monthly appearing medical and related periodicals, clinical studies, trials, research reports, etc., cannot be absorbed by any doctor or scientist due to their tremendous huge volume. The reviews providing minimal relief for that information crisis, despite from every effort, the utilization factor of the available information volume only estimated at a maximum ten percent.

Many other point of view can be enumerated, however the mentioned problems are the chief factors as inhibitor effect for the advancement for this very complex scientific and practical field.

Practical Approach

This paper has the purpose to outline in brief what all be the direction, in order to improve the system.

There are several main parameters, which can be made workable above the mentioned goal.

1 – The first priority is the availability of a huge financial source, controlled by one single independent organization of non-public character, managed by a Non-Business Oriented CEO or Chairman.

2 – That chairman must have enough scientific and practical background to be objective, without any egoistic character, and having firm leadership experience.

3 – The above two properties however are not enough to reach the aforementioned goals. These conceptual contents need to e applied for the long range, or scope, of the project.

The biologic phenomena are under the most complex natural laws in the Universe. The human brain, during the relatively short period of the history of the human existence with respect to the age of our galactic position resulted in the advancement of current technical sciences. It has been identified with other billions and billions of different galaxies, while we are struggling with various illnesses in this world, which is stagnating in nits efforts to resolve fatal diseases. The progress in this direction is very slow, due to the complexity of the biologic phenomena.

Only during the last few years, did appear essential discoveries for medical science. New discoveries, as a new trend, dictate the abolition of the basis of many clinical practices, since the molecular biology has opened a new door to the atrium for the elimination of the human sufferings. It has been, since the period of the Greek philosophers in whom existed a dream to heal the human body. Interestingly, it was by them advocated, holistic views, which rapidly are penetrating the current medical practices.

We have to recognize the difficulties to consider every patient from holistic points of view. There are many so-called 'healers' preying upon the ignorance on the large part of the big masses who are victimized and intellectually abused by their religious beliefs. This wide trend causes difficulties for the practitioner doctors, since the medically, poorly-educated patient cannot have enough trust in doctors. The 'natural treatments' trend proliferates in a very extended manner.

Behind this negative trend is only a financial egoistic interest, which compromises certain well-proven healing methods utilizing homeopathic remedies. They, however, cannot replace the existing pharmaceutical products. The pharmaceutical industry has been developed from herbalistic knowledge, whereby during the beginning of the 18th century European chemists analyzed and later synthesized the acting elements of herbs. This was the birth of synthetical medicines, the current pharmaceutical industry.

Synthesis of Sciences

If the three above-mentioned parameters can be satisfied, then it is possible to establish a medical university with diversified clinics, providing for the doctors and nurses such financial status that they can devote their full intellectual talents for the patients, liberating them from the financial dependency upon the big business in order to survive. Satisfying this requirement, the doctors and nurses will have enough time to update their knowledge because they do not need to fight for a living.

The afore-mentioned university shall have sophisticated facilities to serve the doctors and nurses intellectual needs and assure their continuous education. The clinics shall be organized in such a way that every existing medical specialty will be represented by an institute, led by a professor. The various institutes shall have continuous and direct cooperation under the management of a certain number of professors who will constitute an advisory board. The task and function of that board is to advise all institutes concerning their patients under treatment in each given institute. This system eliminates known major discrepancies wherein patients must run from one doctor to another, or from one hospital to another in order to receive the best believed, or hoped for, treatment.

One can recognize that money becomes not the subject and goal of investment, it is only a tool to provide the best available, updated treatment for the patients.

Not an easy task, however, is to select the doctors and members of clinics for the indicated positions. If this concept would be advertised in advance, a certain percentage of candidates would be willing to be admitted, due to the unusual good financial compensation system. The moral standing of the future staff must also be on the highest level.

A long range contract for each doctor and nurse would be the assurance that they will never face any lay-offs, except in the most extreme cases. Beside the yearly, regular compensation, many additional financial incentives would be available for every one in the university. The doctors would be provided royalties from their lectures and education activities because the university would be part of a world-wide, extended system, also owned and financed by the same organization.

The establishment of the bio-engineering university under the same umbrella will be connected with basic and clinical laboratories, resulting sooner or later in new discoveries, the subject of patents and royalties.

The above clinical complex needs certain amounts of living space with each clinic utilizing 25 to 30 beds. There will be sophisticated laboratories serving the clinical requirements, which would eliminate the necessity to send tissue, blood, and other specimens and samples to different outside laboratories in various parts of the country.

To reach the highest quality of treatment, the lab work, instruments, and equipment will be subject to the availability of funds. In this case, it is a minor problem. The major concern is to find the well-qualified personnel.

Due to the financial strength of the Trust, the most updated technology regarding international communications would be used. The planned professional television studio will be connected world-wide to the sister universities. The university-owned, private television station can realize the most advanced tele-medicine. The technology has already matured.

The university complex, under the same top management, represents the medical school, diversified clinics, basic research, and clinical laboratories with the most advanced diagnostic and therapy equipment. The best expertise will be provided by the bio-engineering university.

If we consider the financial difficulties that the hospitals currently are facing, for example, in order to treat brain cancer, there needs to be a cyclotron, which comes with an enormous cost. The Positron Emission Tomography, digital mammography, and various radiology equipment for tissue evaluation and basic research, requires numerous types of electron microscopes, so a huge capital investment would be needed and very few institutes can afford them.

The accreditation requirements are also related to financial parameters. The servicing personnel, as well as the doctors and all others, must have the highest qualification, therefore the financial compensation plays an important role.

Two sister universities are under work in Switzerland and in Hungary. In Switzerland, there are plans for a European Center for Post-Doctoral Fellowship, which will be directed from Florida. In Hungary, there is to be a medical school in the English language, mostly for foreign students, also directed from Florida.

Various clinics in Switzerland and Hungary need not necessarily be located in the same area. Each shall be considered for special climatic parameters: the availability of thermal water, with special mineral contents, for rheumatic disorders, for heart and circulatory and gynecologic problems. In Switzerland, there are highly specialized thermal baths in different parts of the Alpines. As interesting historical records show, Julius Caesar often visited the Bath in Baden, close to Zurich, to supplement his health.

In Hungary, there are special baths, developed from the period of Turkish Imperium, several centuries ago, and where there are highly-skilled doctors for thalasso therapy.

One can recognize that this type of university conglomerate represents the holistic approach, since all available proven healing methods can be applied on the most advanced scientific level, avoiding any quackery and misrepresentation.

It may also be mentioned that the subject organization has direct contact in China with universities and research centers, therefore, there are available proven methods from Chinese medicine. The domination of the pharmaceutical synthetic, products-oriented industries exercise hidden, unintended inhibitor factors, due to the profit-related investment objectives.

The technical operation in Europe will be centralized in Switzerland. The computer international network center will be placed in China. All data continuously will be fed into the central services system in China as it is received from Florida and from Godollo, Hungary, so all can have access to the necessary selected data.

By the latest technology (ITT/IBM) conferences, business or

scientific meetings can be organized by tele-communications. Therefore, the foreign chief officers do not need to travel to the headquarters. The conferences can be held before a big screen, projected in the local Godollo, Hungry, China, or United States facilities. This kind of system requires a very substantial capital investment, however the Trust has enough financial strength to build up the most updated technical center.

As an example, the company, Informatic, has a crucial role to gather information both in the scientific realm and the business territory. In Godollo, Hungary, is a planned a special institute, linked to Florida, employing Hungarian expertise, whose German and English language knowledge will qualify them for that very essential position.

All employees will have five year renewable contracts with very attractive yearly salaries and fringe benefits. The fringe benefits are health insurance for the employee and family members living in the same household, paid vacations, and additional bonuses from the international profit-producing business income, based upon certain chart-directed percentages.

Since the business-produced profit will be reverted in the Hungarian enterprise, the source of necessary capital always will be available, without hurting the U.S.A. and China capital requirements.

Unfortunately, he became very sickly and finally went into the hospital for the remainder of his days. But, he made me promise that I would continue to fulfill his mission to establish that research hospital. He left me with all the information and documents for the Trust.

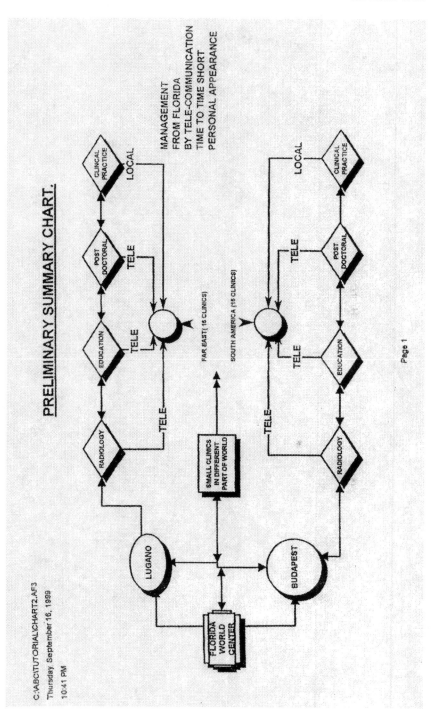

C:\ABC\TUTORIAL\CHART2.AF3
Thursday September 16, 1999
10:41 PM

PRELIMINARY SUMMARY CHART.

CLINICAL PRACTICE

LOCAL

POST DOCTORAL

TELE

EDUCATION

TELE

RADIOLOGY

TELE

TELE

MANAGEMENT
FROM FLORIDA
BY TELE-COMMUNICATION
TIME TO TIME SHORT
PERSONAL APPEARANCE

FAR EAST(15 CLINICS)

SOUTH AMERICA (15 CLINICS)

LOCAL

CLINICAL PRACTICE

TELE

POST DOCTORAL

EDUCATION

TELE

RADIOLOGY

TELE

SMALL CLINICS
IN DIFFERENT
PART OF WORLD

LUGANO

BUDAPEST

FLORIDA
WORLD
CENTER

Page 1

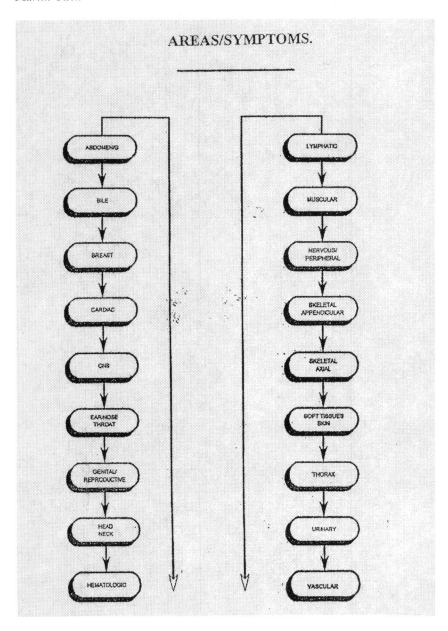

AREAS/SYMPTOMS.

OVERSIGHT.

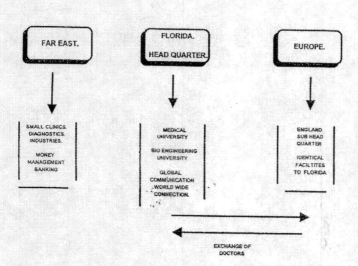

FAR EAST.	FLORIDA. HEAD QUARTER.	EUROPE.

| SMALL CLINICS. DIAGNOSTICS. INDUSTRIES. MONEY MANAGEMENT BANKING | MEDICAL UNIVERSITY BIO ENGINEERING UNIVERSITY GLOBAL COMMUNICATION WORLD WIDE CONNECTION. | ENGLAND SUB HEAD QUARTER IDENTICAL FACILTITES TO FLORIDA |

EXCHANGE OF DOCTORS

SMALL CLINICS OWNED BY THE SAME COMPANY THROUGH
SUBSIDIARY SYSTEM.

THE PROFESSIONAL MANAGEMENT OF
BOTH UNIVSERSITY AND INDUSTRIAL
FIELD IS TO BE FROM FLORIDA AND
FROM ENGLAND

IN HUNGARY AND SWITZERLAND TO BE SET UP IDENTICAL
FACILITIES AS TO FLORIDA, HOWEVER, IN HUNGARY
THE COST OF LABOR IS NOT MORE THAN 30% RESPECT
TO WESTERN EUROOPEAN COUNTRIES, BUT THE DOCTORS
ARE VERY WELL SKILLED.

GENERAL REVIEW OF MEDICAL SCHOOL AND BIO ENGINEERING
(SEPT. 1999).

DRM UNIVERSITY is to be composed by MEDICAL SCHOOL (including Clinics) and BIO ENGINEERING UNIVERSITY under the same theoretical and practical management. The purpose of this two higher education institutions is to utilize and melting together a decade ago independent two disciplines and improving the efficacy of the HEALTH SCIENCE for the benefit of the patients.

The medical activity, the function of physicians is more and more connected with sophisticated instruments and equipments due to the incredible fast advancement of the application of technical (electro-technical and mechanical) tools, which are nowadays available and serving the needs of physicians.

The major problem emerges from the quick obsolescence of referred instruments and equipments because the speedy advancement in field of molecular biology, rapid progress of discovery of new genes fast transforms previously used treatment methods, what the physicians can follow only very slowly, due to the time requirements for reading, disseminating understanding and applying the new results for the daily medical practice.

The education process of the new medical doctors nowadays requires new type of system to let absorb the knowledges, strongly related to other disciplines, which not long time ago still belonged to different professionals areas, like engineering, physics etc.

Therefore the necessity to combine the various disciplines under the same theoretical and practical management requires the melting of the medical school (clinics) and special engineering.

GENERAL ORGANIZATIVE STRUCTURE.

This paper refers only to the

RADIOLOGY MANAGEMENT PROBLEMS,

for the purpose to have further refinement and set up the final and correct structure.

The first major task is the

PROJECT PLANNING OF THE DIAGNOSTIC IMAGING DEPARTMENT.

Certain common step in the planning process are necessary to ensure the success of construction project of the diagnostic imaging department. Determining the need for the project, analyzing requirements for equipments, space and personnel and budgeting for the project. Scheduling and designing the various aspects of the project. Engineering the construction phase and implementation with follow-up.

Cost-benefit analysis.

Communication with key staff members of the health care institutions and the members of the design and construction team.

Analysis of potential project's equipments, space and personnel needs.

Outline the general principles of design, planning and budgeting applied to the specific needs of imaging department.

DESIGN SPECIFICATION BY MODALITY.

Modalities are:
DIAGNOSTIC RADIOLOGY
MAMMOGRAPHY
SPECIAL PROCEDURES
CARDIAC CATHETERIZATION
ULTRASOUND
COMPUTED TOMOGRAPHY SCANNING
MAGNETIC RESONANCE IMAGING
NUCLEAR MEDICINE (CYCLOTRON)
POSITRON EMISSION TECHNOLOGY
BONE DENSITOMETRY
OTHER NOT LISTED ITEMS

****

The enclosed CHART summarizes the international aspects of the RADIOLOGY AND RELATED SUBCATEGORIES.

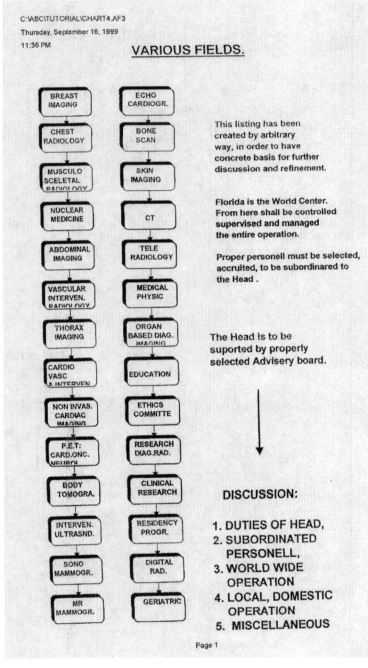

C:\ABC\TUTORIAL\CHART4.AF3
Thursday, September 16, 1999
11:36 PM

VARIOUS FIELDS.

BREAST IMAGING	ECHO CARDIOGR.
CHEST RADIOLOGY	BONE SCAN
MUSCULO SCELETAL RADIOLOGY	SKIN IMAGING
NUCLEAR MEDICINE	CT
ABDOMINAL IMAGING	TELE RADIOLOGY
VASCULAR INTERVEN. RADIOLOGY	MEDICAL PHYSIC
THORAX IMAGING	ORGAN BASED DIAG. IMAGING
CARDIO VASC & INTERVEN	EDUCATION
NON INVAS. CARDIAC IMAGING	ETHICS COMMITTE
P.E.T: CARD.ONC. NEURO	RESEARCH DIAG.RAD.
BODY TOMOGRA.	CLINICAL RESEARCH
INTERVEN. ULTRASND.	RESIDENCY PROGR.
SONO MAMMOGR.	DIGITAL RAD.
MR MAMMOGR.	GERIATRIC

This listing has been created by arbitrary way, in order to have concrete basis for further discussion and refinement.

Florida is the World Center. From here shall be controlled supervised and managed the entire operation.

Proper personell must be selected, accruited, to be subordinared to the Head .

The Head is to be suported by properly selected Advisery board.

DISCUSSION:

1. DUTIES OF HEAD,
2. SUBORDINATED PERSONELL,
3. WORLD WIDE OPERATION
4. LOCAL, DOMESTIC OPERATION
5. MISCELLANEOUS

Page 1

158

BIOG1015.01

DRM HAS ESTABLISHED IN FLORIDA A MAJOR PRIVATE MEDICAL UNIVERSITY IN PALM BEACH COUNTY,

UNIVERSITY TO BE CONNECTED WITH SWITZERLAND, IN AREA OF LUGANO (TICINO), WHERE THE SAME WILL BE BUILT, TO BE MANAGED FROM FLORIDA.

ALREADY HAS BEEN ORGANIZED WORLD WIDE THE MOST EXPERIENCED ONCOLOGIST, 1500 OF THEM, WHO WILL SERVING THE REFERENCED UNIVERSITIES, WHEREBY ALREADY ONE OF THE WORLD KNOWN ONCOLOGIST, PROFESSOR NABHOLZ, CANADA, NOW PROFESSOR IN CALIFORNIA, UCLA, PREVIOUSLY IN EDMONTON UNIVERSITY AND DR. PROF. VOGEL, FORMER PROFESSOR IN MIAMI UNIVERSITY, FROM PLANTATION, FLORIDA ASSIGNED TO BE THE CHIEF SCIENTIST OF THE UNIVERSITIES.

NOW UNDER ARRANGEMENT TO PURCHASE TWO LOCAL HOSPITAL,BECOMING PART OF THE MEDICAL UNIVERSITY.

DRM has DIRECT CONNECTION TO THE VATICAN IN ROME, THE MODALITIES OF IN LUGANO CONCERNING THE POST DOCTORAL FELLOWSHIP PROGRAM ALREADY HAS BEEN ARRANGED BY "HIS EMINENCE, EDMUND CASIMIR, CARDINAL SZOKA, CARDINALE PRESIDENTE, PONTIFICIA COMMISSIONE, PER LO STATO DELLA CITTA DEL VATICANO" (Communication by italian language, due the Switzera Italiana, Ticino, Lugano),

The negotiation in Ticino are already in good progress. The concrete plan is to establish in Ticino a major Medical Research and Post Doctoral Fellow Center. The Post Doctoral Fellow Program is planned to be performed by already selected and agreed Doctors, Professors, in Zurich, Basel, Genf, California, New York, Boston, by satellite Tele-Medicine System, therefore unnecessary to be continuously present the professor staff in Ticino, due to the Tel-Medicine (Motorola/IBM system).
      This intellectual international center will generate very substantial foreign participation (by the function and task of 1500 oncologist World-Wide, se above Prof. Nabholtz, California).

The central issues are the Cancer and Wilson Syndrome, which one is one of the most devastating illness World-Wide. University of Milano and the Tumor Institute in Milano planned to be involved in the Ticino Scientific Center. For foreign participants, who are not speaking well english already has been agreed with the English Language Institute in Lugano to assist.(Interestingly that Institute has been organized by a teachers couple from North Carolina USA, for the purpose to serve the children of the Americans, and others, residing and working in Switzerland).

Cancer is well known illness. Wilson Syndrome however, not well known. It is a gene related disease. Certain genes missing by birth in the children's body. Very interestingly such children have fantastic level of ability to learn languages and perform music, however have no any kind of ability to understand mathematics and

Martin Olson

BIOG1015.01
other real disciplines. A 14 years age of kid can learn
simultaneously two foreign languages and have the judgement
ability alike a 40 years old experienced person. They cannot
absorb anything else, than language and music. That kids are
aware of their illness, entirely understood and know that they
have very limited life span. The progress in this field is very
rapid.

The gene research is our major area. This is why the referenced
University related persons organizing World-Wide the expertise
for our centralized Institutional management.

As to latest updated medical check up,(April, 2000) DRM
is in excellent health conditions.

Al-Dawlia and Rapid Seven Ltd. has been associated for the
organization of major sub research center in Saudi Arabia and the
Post Doctoral Fellowship, to be centralized in Switzerland.   In
The history of the Saudi Arabia plan going back to the Kuwait war
period, whereas my Daughter has organized it.

Ticino has been consultation at the local government and already
there are various site selections where Private Institute
planned to set up.

In field of Gene therapy in USA has been set up an affiliation
with NOVARTIS (merged former Ciba,Sandoz, Switzerland), whereas
the vital organs of little pigs,(heart, lung, pancreas, breast,
brain, etc.) by cloning methods can be humanized therefore the
transplants will not be rejected, unlike the regular tissues,
received form an other human donor. Additionally the cost factors
will be much less. This experiments are already in phase of
clinical trials and within 4-5 years will be in the medical
practice.

In this short letter impossible to outline the whole system, and
the performed job which has started about 10 years ago and now
matured, however upon request can be furnished more details.

Sincerely;

DR. SANDOR MIHALY

160

The above rendering is a study of the International Medical University. The design is similar to a medical center in the U.S.A. This study is to have all the medical departments as outlined by Dr. Mihaly but an additional research center directed by John Heimerman, known as the Anthropological Research Center located in Salt Lake City, Utah. Also to incorporate the new medical technologically of "NANO Medicine".

The above study is of the main entrance to the Medical University. The basic study is to control movement of personal, material and services and to allow change and expansion. Gross floor area approximately 150,000 m^2, which would include the Anthropological Research Center.

CHAPTER TEN

India Notes

THE TRUST HAS MANY agents around the world, and since the use of the Japanese Notes is very political, and projects are demanding a start up, the Chairman had decided to have his agents in India be in contact with the State Bank of India. The State Bank of India agreed and the Doctor issued a forty million dollar promissory note to the State Bank of India. The State Bank of India, in turn, would issue and have printed forty $1,000,000 notes from the American Bank Note Company in New York. Each note to have a cusip or an I.S.I.N. registered number. Since the cusip number, controlled by Standard and Poors, can only be issued to American issued notes, and the State Bank of India notes are to be issued from offshore, hence out of U.S.A., this would mean that only I.S.I.N. numbers could be used. The I.S.I.N. numbers are controlled by Euroclear in Brussels as an all sure issue. Also, this would mean they would be under their control as they are registered in Brussels and not in the U.S.A.

The State Bank of India then started to issue the orders to American Bank Note Company starting in November of 1994. One of the orders was that Martin Olson be authorized to pick up the printed notes, not issues with a registration number, and deliver them to the Chairman in Zurich, Switzerland. I was given copies of all orders from the State Bank of India to the American Bank Note Company. The Chairman requested, before the decision to take the notes to Zurich, that I find a security firm in New York that could hold them until he came back to New York. I was in contact with Prudential Securities and they started to request that they control the securities, not the Trust. This was denied.

Smith Barney and Company tried to do the same thing, but when the Trust refused, Prudential called the S.E.C. At this point, the notes printed by American Bank Note Company were only paper and of no value until the I.S.I.N. numbers were issued.

So in January of 1995, I went to New York at the request of the Chairman, and by the authorization of the State Bank of India. My purpose was to go to the American Bank Note Company to pick up the blank notes. This meeting was prearranged with the offices of the Note Company for me to pick up the forty, million dollar notes, plus eight, two-year bearer notes, ordered by the State Bank of India. I had instructions from the State Bank of India to act in their behalf to Take possession of the notes and deliver them to the Chairman in Zurich, Switzerland, the following day. During the trip, from the airport to the city, I was very leery of the meeting, and tried to analyze all the details in my mind, because I did not trust the United States Government or its agents, such as the Secret Service. I also reflected back some seven years previously to my last encounter with the Secret Service in Washington, D.C. regarding the Japanese bearer notes, and what the Secret Service told me about the Chairman, that he would finally deliver and start working on the projects the Chairman had decided to undertake with the use of the Japanese Notes.

So I decided to keep the meeting at 10:00 a.m. in the Offices of the American Bank Note Company. The Chairman designed and wrote the wording of the notes, that design and the final wording were done along European lines.

I had with me copies of the State Bank of India orders, correspondence between the Chairman and the Bank Note Company and myself, as well as copies of letters from Smith Barney and Prudential securities. The notes would have no I.S.I.N. numbers from Euroclear in Brussels as of that date until the notes were delivered to them. When I was at the American Bank Note Company to pick up the notes, the Secret Service was there and made their presence known. The Secret Service jumped the gun by not checking all the facts, instead only accepting the word of Prudential Securities who attempted to take control of the Indian Notes, and put the Chairman and me under investigation.

After approximately two years, the trial, which was controlled by U.S. picked attorneys, put me on probation, and the Chairman in prison for one year, followed by probation. The reason the Chairman was willing to spend the one year in jail was because he would not disclose any of the details with regard to these notes, or the use of the money, nor the Japanese Secret MacArthur Fund Notes, all to protect the Trust.

The final chapter on this fiasco was that the Government of India issued proof that the State Bank of India is sued notes, were legitimate, and the Chairman was now waiting for the U.S. Justice System to have the entire case removed, and all charges dropped. At a loss of three years of money, time to try to stop the Chairman, and bury the information on the MacArthur Funds, we later discovered that someone printed an I.S.I.N. number on the notes after we were charged. This was highlighted by two prints of the notes; one with no number, and one with a number, as a government exhibit. Also the probation officer, and their statement, so stated that no numbers were issued because only Euroclear could issue an offshore note.

There was additional evidence that the Secret Service and Justice Department concealed evidence just to get a conviction but now, more importantly, that the Chairman was put out of commission because of the Japanese Secret MacArthur Fund Notes. In fact, the Justice Department told me in conferences that there were no Japanese MacArthur Notes, and, therefore, they would not discuss them or the amount of non-existent notes moved to the U.S. with the approval of the U.S. Customs or transferred to Japan with the approval of U.S. Customs.

The Justice Department and Secret Service are good at covering up the past at anyone's cost and lying about it. Washington is very good at this. One has to have iron shoes for undertaking this kind of journey.

cory

C:\WP51\BANK\DRMPN_1.SBI   PAGE NO.1.

PROMISSORY NOTE.

PLACE:VADUZ,LIECHTENSTEIN
SERIAL NO.:A-01
REGISTER NO:378
DATE OF ISSUE:OCTOBER 20,1994.
DATE OF MATURITY:AS TO CONDITIONS ON THE REVERSE SIDE.

FOR VALUE RECEIVED,I,DR. ███████████,IDENTIFIED BY THE ATTACHED
AFFIDAVIT,DO HEREBY,IRREVOCABLY AND UNCONDITIONALLY, WITHOUT
RECOURSE,PROTEST OR NOTIFICATION OF PROTEST,PROMISE TO PAY
AGAINST THIS PROMISSORY NOTE THE SUM OF 40 (FOURTY) MILLION
DOLLARS IN LAWFUL TENDER OF THE UNITED STATES OF AMERICA TO STATE
BANK OF INDIA,MADAME CAMA ROAD,P.O.BOX 10121,BOMBAY, AS TO
CONDITIONS ON THE REVERSE SIDE.

THE FOREGOING AMOUNT IS PAYABLE NET OF ANY FEES,TAXES,COST OR
OTHER DEDUCTIONS,IMPOSTS,LEVIES OR DUTIES,PRESENT AND FUTURE,OF
ANY NATURE,WHATSOEVER IMPOSED OR AFFIXED UNDER THE LAWS OF
LIECHTENSTEIN OR ANY POLITICAL SUBDIVISION THEREOF OR THEREIN IN
CONNECTION WITH THE ISSUANCE,ENDORSEMENT OR PAYMENT OF THIS
PROMISSORY NOTE AND,I,THE ISSUER,IRREVOCABLY AND UNCONDITIONALLY
INDEMNIFY THE PAYEE ACCORDINGLY.

THE TERMS AND CONDITIONS OF THIS PROMISSORY NOTE ARE TO BE
GOVERNED AND CONSTRUED IN ACCORDANCE WITH THE DOCUMENTARY CREDITS
INSTRUMENTS AS APPROVED BY THE INTERNATIONAL CHAMBER OF COMMERCE,
PARIS AS TO BROCHURE I.C.C 500 AND AS TO COLLECTION ORDER 322 FOR
CLEAN COLLECTION.

THE FAILURE OF THE HOLDER OF THIS PROMISSORY NOTE TO EXERCISE ANY
OF ITS RIGHTS HEREUNDER SHALL NOT CONSTITUTE ANY APPROBATION
THEREOF IN ANY INSTANCE DURING THE RELEVANT PERIOD.

ALL RIGHTS ARISING FROM THE OWNERSHIP OF THIS PROMISSORY NOTE ARE
NON TRASNFERABLE.

SIGNATURE OF DR.███████████
AS TO ATTACHED AFFIDAVIT.

भारतीय स्टेट बैंक
मुख्य शाखा
पोस्ट बाक्स नं. 430
11, संसद मार्ग,
नई दिल्ली-110001
तार : थीसस

State Bank of India
Main Branch
Post Box No. 450
11, Sansad Marg,
New Delhi -110001
Telegram : THISTLE

क०/No.

दिनांक/Date

" RELEVENT EXTRACT OF B.O.D. MEETING HELD ON 26.9.94
AT S.B.I., SANSAD MARG, NEW DELHI.

BE AND IS HEREBY RESOLVED THAT MR. S. PANIHATI, DY
GENERAL MANAGER AND MR. ASHOK NAYAR, ASSTT. GENERAL
MANAGER OF FOREIGN EXCHANGE DEPARTMENT be authorised
to jointly execute/assigned/accept/issue Promissory
Notes of the bank for value over ten million
U.S.Dollors (10,000,000.00 USD) upto fifty million
U.S.Dollors (50,000,000.00 USD) in the normal accepted
practices under the Banking Regulations Act 1949.

Further resolved that Notes issued/ accepted as above
shall be binding on State Bank of India and deemed to
be issued/accepted by it.

For An On Behalf Of The S.B.I. BOARD.

(A.K. SEN)
Dy. Managing Director
North Zone "

भारतीय स्टेट बैंक
मुख्य शाखा
पोस्ट बाक्स नं• 430
11, संसद मार्ग,
नई दिल्ली-110001
तार : थीसल

State Bank of India

Main Branch
Post Box No. 430
11, Sansad Marg,
New Delhi - 110001
Telegram : THISTLE

कृ०/No.

दिनांक/Date

TO HAND OF : MR .JOSEPH A.NAPOLITANO   NOV 1,1994
             VICE PRESIDENT,
             AMERICAN BANK NOTE COMPANY
             51 WEST 52 ND STREET
             NEW YORK   10019
             U.S.A
             FAX :212 582 9332
             PHONE :212 582 -9200

DEAR MR NAPOLITANO ,

AS TO ARRANGEMENT , MADE BY DR. ▓▓▓▓▓▓▓ , BUCHHOLZSTRASSE
47,8053 ZURICH , SWITZERLAND,WHO ACT ON BEHALF OF OUR BANK , YOU
FIND ENCLOSED THE FOLLOWING DOCUMENTS , PROPERLY EXECUTED AS TO
REQUESTED BY THE LAWS OF OUR BANK .

1.-IMPRESSION OF SEAL OF STATE BANK OF INDIA (THREE TIMES)ON
   STATIONERY FORM OF AMERICAN BANK NOTE COMPANY .

2.-THE NAMES , SIGNATURES AND TITLE OF TWO BANK OFFICERS, AND THE
   SPECIMEN OF SIGNATURES EACH ONE THREE TIMES , ON TWO
   STATIONERIES FORM OF AMERICAN BANK NOTE COMPANY .

3.-COMPLETE INSTRUCTIONS AND ORDER TO PRINT AND HANDLE SENIOR BANK
   NOTES .

4.-IN THE EVENT IF THE TEXT ENCLOSED ARE NOT CLEAR OR ENOUGH DR
   ▓▓▓▓▓▓▓▓ WILL SUPPLY PROPER INSTRUCTION ON BEHALF OF STATE
   ▓▓▓▓ OF INDIA.

YOURS SINCERELY :

MR S.PANIHATI
DY GENERAL MANAGER

167

भारतीय स्टेट बैंक
मुख्य शाखा
पोस्ट बास नं. 430
11, संसद मार्ग,
नई दिल्ली-110001
द्वार : थीसल

State Bank of India
Main Branch
Post Box No. 430
11, Sansad Marg,
New Delhi - 110001
Telegram : THISTLE

कo/No.

दिनांक/Date

**GOVERNMENT
EXHIBIT**
GX-5
95 Cr. 181

REFERENCE NUMBER 157/MB-FX/94 IN OUR FILE

TO HANDS OF : MR JOSEPH A. NAPOLITANO , VICE PRESIDENT
AMERICAN BANK NOTE COMPANY
41 WEST 52 ND STREET
NEW YORK , NEW YORK 10019
FAX 212 582 9332

DATE NOV.15,1994.

DEAR MR NAPOILTANO :

THE TELEPHONE CONVERSATION FROM YESTERDAY , BETWEEN MR A.K.SEN ,
MANAGING DIRECTOR OF S.B.I. (NORTH ZONE)AND MR JERRY FAULKNER ,
MANAGER STANDARD & POORS , NEW YORK , CLEARED THAT THE LAW DO NOT
REQUEST ANY CUSIP OR OTHER NUMBERS PRINTED ON THE NOTES . SINCE THE
NOTES ARE NOT REGISTERED IN THE U.S.A. THEREFORE IN OUR INSTRUCTION
, REF .NO 157/MB-FX/94 AS OF NOV.1.1994,PAR NO.2.13 SHALL BE
DELETED AND PLEASE TO FOLLOW THE INSTRUCTIONS TO BE GIVEN BY DR
████████████████ ,BY FAX FROM SWITZERLAND , TO WHERE THE PRINTED NOTES
SHALL BE DELIVERED BY YOUR COMPANY.

SINCERELY YOURS:

MR.S.PANIHATI
DY . GENERAL MANAGER

MR.ASHOK NAYAR
ASSTT.GENERAL MANAGER
OF FOREIGN EXCHANGE DEPARTMENT

STAMP OF S.B.I.

101d

TOTAL P.01

भारतीय स्टेट बैंक
मुख्य शाखा
पोस्ट बाक्स नं॰ 430
11, संसद मार्ग,
नई दिल्ली-110001
तार : थीसल

State Bank of India
Main Branch
Post Box No. 430
11, Sansad Marg,
New Delhi - 110001
Telegram : THISTLE

क्र॰/No. MB-1/960/95   दिनांक/Date Jan.02, 1995

AMERICAN BANK NOTE COMPANY
MR. JOSEPH A. NAPOLITANO, V.P.
51 WEST 52ND STREET
14TH FLOOR
NEW YORK, N.Y. 10019
U.S.A.

Dear Mr. Napolitano:

In reference to bearer senior notes, as to a 40 million
US Dollars' issue, in form of one million US dollars
denominations, Total of Forty (40) notes plus eight (8)
notes, this latter ones for the purpose of eventual
replacement in case of necessity, notes have been issued as
of November 8, 1994, maturing as of November 8, 1996, with,
by Euroclear Provided ISIN XS0054722615 Number, as to
advised by Dr. ███████████████, our representative
(Buchholzstrasse 47, 5, Stock, 8053 Zurich, Switzerland) it
is hereby confirmed, that

    MR. MARTIN GEORGE OLSON
    IDENTIFIED BY US PSSPORT NUMBER :041193867
    EXPIRES AS OF 6. OCT. 1995

has been fully authorized to represent our bank one time,
to retrieve the above referred bearer notes from American
Bank Note Company, against receipt, whereby to the package
of notes shall be enclosed an original document, signed
officially by American Bank note Company, and Mr. Olson,
that the notes have been retrieved by Mr.Olson by our one
time representative.

This authorization expires on the same day, when Mr. OLSON
has received the notes from American Bank Note Company.
Thank you for your good services.

for STATE BANK OF INDIA

S. PANIHATI
DY. GENERAL MANAGER

ASHOK NAYAR
ASSTT. GENL.MANAGER OF
FOREIGN EXCHANGE DEPARTMENT

169

CHAPTER ELEVEN

Power and Control

WHO CONTROLS THIS WORLD or tries to? There are two large groups who operate as a secret society: one, is in Europe, and is known as the Bilderberg Group and the second, which is in the U.S.A., is the Council on Foreign Regulations (CFR).

There is a major difference in their mode of operation. The Bilderberg Group, or Banks Club, tries to assist countries, and does not become involved directly in military operations. The CFR Group, in the U.S.A., has a motto to wage economic war against the world in the name of market share for American products, In 1995, it was recommended that the intelligence agencies be used for industrial espionage to benefit U.S. companies. There are presently approximately 4,200 members coming from corporations, academia, charities, government, law and media. Allen Dulles was the first president of CFR in 1950, who afterwards became the Director of the United States Center Intelligence Agency. Many of the U.S. Presidents and their appointed heads of governmental departments are CFR members.

The above information about CFR is from "Who really runs the world" by Thom Burnett and Alex Games, 2007..

It is strange that when the CFR was formed in 1950, it was to increase the U.S. economy, and now, as of 2007, that method is not working. Most products are made in India and China. So what has changed? Nothing! It is all about money and greed. It always has been that way.

Looking back to Dr. Sandor Mihaly, after learning about the CFR Group, it helped me to solve a question I had as to why the U.S.A. would try to indict the Doctor on trumped up charges in New York in 1998 regarding the India Notes and put him jail for approximately one year. Now I think I have finally found the answer. It helps to recall the three major projects that the Chairman had control over and was working on in 1998:

Project 1:

The trust had control of most of the Secret MacArthur Funds, as outlined in the earlier chapters, since the 1980's. These secret funds were from the end of the Japanese War with the U.S.A. President Truman refused to allow Russia in on the rebuilding of Japan. So the President arranged to fund the entire rebuilding of Japan, which was managed by General MacArthur.

As each payment was made, the U.S.A. received as a guarantee notes to repay the U.S. taxpayer plus interest over a period of time. Now comes Richard Nixon who worked with Thomas Dewey who represented Japan in Washington. Tom Dewey gave the Japanese account to Nixon. Now Nixon wanted to run for the Presidency of the U.S.A. and needed funds, and Japan wanted to get rid of the notes and not repay the U.S.A. So, Nixon arranged to have the notes laundered thru the Japanese banks so that the guarantee to repay with interest was changed to, "It may repay, if Japan approves."

Now the US taxpayer is screwed out of 600 billion dollars plus interest, or a total of over one trillion U.S. dollars, and it is all kept secret by the Secret Service. I was involved, as was shown in previous chapters, as a courier, and I transported 16 billion dollars of notes to Japan, with the approval of the Secret Service and U.S. Customs Office.

Project 2:

The Chairman, Dr. Mihaly, worked on providing a 50 billion USD grant to China thru the Bank of China, and that would be used to repay the World Bank debt and could be rolled over nine times, or a total of 500 billion dollars, to make China a world power. Papers were all drawn and ready for signatures.

Project 3:

The Chairman, Dr. Mihaly, worked on a loan arrangement with India to provide funds for the medical field, secured by bonds. The bonds were printed in New York but without the certificate numbers on the bonds. If the bonds had the numbers printed on them, they would be illegal in the USA as a foreign security, so the printed bonds were only a piece of paper without the certificate numbers.

The Chairman and I were detained by the Secret Service. I was released but the Chairman had to stand trial. The U.S. Attorney wanted all the details of the trust and its involvement in its many projects. The Doctor refused to answer any questions, so, as mentioned earlier, he went to jail for one year. After the trial, the court system told me that the U.S. Attorneys had added the certificate numbers to the bonds themselves, which they now said made them illegal notes. I told the Doctor later, but it was too late. Upon his release, he went right back to work on the India and the China funding.

Now this was late 1999 and on December 2001, the Doctor died of an aneurysm of the heart. So, currently, all the MacArthur Notes are silent, and the China funding is gone was well as the India funding. How convenient. The current trustees in Switzerland will do nothing, as the doctor had all the knowledge and drive.

So, now, it makes sense about the trumped-up charges to the Doctor, it kept all the secrets safe, and China in check. Except, I wrote a book in 2002 called "Iron Shoes," which I had published covering the MacArthur Notes and the India Notes.

The Doctor died on December 13, 2001. His wife, Maria Mihaly, now deceased, told me that on December 12, 2001, he became very ill. A doctor came and told them that he had an aneurysm of the heart. Maria wanted the Chairman to go to the hospital immediately. He refused and died the following day. I was his closest friend, and he knew what was done to him, and he accepted his fate. After the Doctor's death, the Swiss Trustees never called Maria Mihaly, nor made sure she was cared for. The State of Florida took care of Maria Mihaly completely, including treatment for her cancer.

"Morals and responsibility walk hand in hand with capacity and power."

G. Holland

CHAPTER TWELVE

Personal Notes

"The world's disease is a giant whirlpool of evil and weakness which draws its victims down to doom, even as they struggle for freedom. The sins of silence and inaction are often blacker than the sins of words and deeds.

"The world's design is by men and women who are producers and consumers living in an ultramodern industrial civilization created by the machine and spanning all the planet. This machine has made all of the world one market, one work shop, one playground, and one great neighborhood whose people are dependent on upon another for livelihood and security. In the end, all the world's children awaken to discover that the machine has made all one family united and indivisible with its members linked by ties of trade, travel, and investment, into a world society, which has been affected in a million hidden ways. This result was clearly not a curse but a boom for the race. The practices of men, in earning a living, put the world together, but the seeds of tragedy lay in some men preaching patriotism, tore the world apart into an ever larger number of political entities, waging tariff wars and arranging wars and diplomatic wars and military wars one against another.

"The power of politics, and politics of power, and the source of the energy, is control and greed. It seems that it will never end. Most people receive the kind of leadership they deserve."

The above description of the world came from a book <u>Design for Power</u> written by Frederick Schuman in 1941, 66 years ago. Nothing has changed.

With all our advancements in technology, and the electronic age, what we have done hasn't worked.

War didn't bring us peace and security.

Agri business didn't feed the world.

A high-tech world didn't bring us leisure times.

Economists didn't level the playing field.

Wealth never trickled down.

Resources are depleted:

Our planet is in critical condition.

Our present is fear based and greed. The great teachings were love based. We have focused on symptoms without understanding their root causes. Fear breeds scarcity, greed, dominance, racism, hate, violence, fundamentalism, and all other "us or them" divisions. The wisdom of love is in conversation, compassion, kindness, caring, sharing and inclusion.

By: "World Wisdom Council"
September 9, 2006, Berlin, Germany

The above sounds like 1941 – power and greed will always be with the world because humans live in it.

The Swiss Trust, with all its power and assets, has done nothing to assist mankind but earn more money for its depositors. If it used only some of the interest from its currency for projects such as hospitals, clinics, and research, it would give great benefit for mankind.

All the research studies that the Doctor did, and my small part in these studies and research, were only used by the Trust as an exercise so that the Trust can show the depositors that they are working on many projects. I was never paid by the Trust. It was my fault for staying with the Doctor but I believed in his mission to build an international research hospital. I also learned a great deal, and I liked the Doctor and his wife.

The Trust had too many restrictions on use of the interest earned and could only be used in very large amounts, which made it difficult to associate the government guarantees required by the Trust.

The Doctor had a long history of medical problems. He had Crohn's disease. He was in the hospital every year since 1956, for treatment of his digestive system. With all these distractions the Doctor kept working on his vision of a biomedical university that would benefit the whole of humanity. The Doctor had to also manage the Trust business, and establish the safe way to finance the university. The Doctor told me many times that he and I have a mission to build the medical university before we leave this earth. He never discussed his illness with me, only business, and never showed any weakness or complained about his discomfort. The only comment he made was at lunch; he would love

French fries and would say that, "It was a good thing that my wife is not here because I love French fries." Oh, well, small pleasures, but I can imagine he suffered later that day.

At our weekly meetings, he would talk about his mother and how religious she was. I asked him if he believed. His answer was that he is a scientist, and everything has to be proven. My answer to him was that "You need faith in the unknown, and with faith you will see miracles happen in your journey of life. I know because it has happened to me."

As stated earlier, the Doctor passed away on December 13, 2001, after an aneurysm of the heart in Riveria Beach, Florida.

* * * * *

In August of 2010, the "World Economic Forum gathered in Tianjm, China to debate the question of finding a new description of a World Order and the future of the global economy.

The current label of 'emerging markets' for developed and underdeveloped countries does not fit anymore. The Global economic landscape is clearly changing as China has become the second largest economy replacing the title held by Japan for the last four decades.

In 1954, the World Government was formed for Europe and was expanded to include North America. This initiative was somewhat driven by joint participation in conflicts and wars.

The following figures represent a quick snapshot of the changing world we live in. For discussion purposes, we should focus not on size, but more so on the new Global co-dependence enhanced by the media and high levels of communication. Most importantly, two of the strongest elements, the Financial and Health sectors, immediately come to mind.

Population World *(000)

	2006	2050
World Total	6,749,700	9.191,300

Population by Country

Africa	987,000	1,997,900
Arab States	335,000	598,500
Asia	4,075,400	5,265,900
Europe	731,000	664,200
Latin America & Caribbean	579,400	769,200
North America	339,800	438,000
Oceana	34,700	48,700
Canada	33,200	42,800
Switzerland	7,500	18,400

In 2006 – Asia had 60.3% of the World Population

In 2050 – Asia projected population 57.3%

World Utilities

World Energy Production/Barrels per day

	1980	2007
Petroleum	63,987,000	84,439,000
North America	14,754,000	15,382,000
Middle East	19,024,000	24,582,000

World Consumption Energy/Barrels Per Day

World Total	63,107,000	82,594,700
North America	20,203,800	25,003,460
Asia	10,729,100	23,341,000

Western Europe	14,322,000	16,307,800

Largest Armed Forces

Number of Armed Forces and Reservists

China	2,105,000	800,000
United States	1,498,000	1,083,000
India	1,288,000	1,155,000
North Korea	1,106,000	4,700,000
Russia	1,027,000	20,000,000
South Korea	687,000	4,500,000

World Leading Exporters & Importers

Exporter	Importer
Germany 1.112 Billion	United States 1,919.4 Billion
United States 1,038.3 Billion	Germany 9086. Billion
China 968.9 Billion	China 791,5 Billion .

Source: New York Times Almanac 2009

CHAPTER THIRTEEN

Conclusion

I was the Doctor's assistant for 15-plus years during his most important time of trying to establish his vision of an international medical university. It was a difficult time for the Doctor due to his medical condition. He worked hard and long hours every day with all the details required for his project. I did my best to assist him while I was caring for my wife dying of cancer. Maybe these trials of life helped us both to work more and push on.

Now that the Doctor is not here physically, it is hoped that someone, or some group, would take on the task of building an international medical university somewhere. It was the Doctor's vision that all doctors, world wide, would have access to the university for the latest and best method to treat their patients at a very low cost. It was also planned that each doctor would have visual access to the professors, and even help direct the medical procedures world wide. It would also be a teaching university with seminars available to everyone.

This true story of Dr. Mihaly is being told so that his vision is not dead and his life's work was not wasted.

"So, while we are alone in our responsibility, we need to give no thought for anything but our own duty and our own little fragment of the Lord's work. The things we cannot do, some other one is waiting and preparing how to do after the work has passed from our hand."
Amen

In all of the Doctor's efforts in his life, he was a faithful servant to the end. Faithfulness as a measure of requirement is not something that can be reached without great effort.

"The certainty that life cannot be long and the probability that it will be shorter than nature allows, ought to waken every man to the active prosecution of whatever he is desirous to perform. It is true that no diligence can ensure success. Death may interrupt the swiftest career, but he who is cut off in the execution of an honest undertaking has at

least the honor of failing in his rank, and has fought the battle though
he missed the victory."   Johnson

Dr. Sandor Mihaly was a loyal, dedicated Chairman of the Swiss
Trust for many years. The Doctor risked everything he had to defend
and keep information about the Trust secret even when he faced going
to j ail on a trumped-up charge that was false. The Doctor's real goal
was to build this international medical university that would benefit
all mankind.

Dr. Sandor Mihaly passed away, leaving his wife, Dr. Maria
(Gabriella), and two children who live in Europe. The Doctor's legacy
reflecting his work in his lifetime was the bringing to light 75 medical
discoveries, which he patented. His love was his medical research. He
was a faithful servant. The Doctor did his best during his lifetime.

You have just read about Dr. Mihaly and the Silent Trust. It also
gave you information about the Swiss Silent Trust involvement with the
secret MacArthur-Japanese notes, which Japan did not have to repay
the U.S. citizens. It informed you of the power of money in the world,
and about control and greed. So, what can the average citizen in the
world do about it or even care about it. The answer, I believe, is that the
average citizen can do nothing but be better than the immoral persons
who have created this depressing abyss for all but the upper echelon who
care nothing for anyone but themselves.

Each individual is to do the "best he or she can" in their life's
struggles. To be honest and display high morals in everything one does
in life, which will show in each person's account before the judgment
seat. The shadows that one casts and the influence one makes, effects
all around them and is a benediction of one's life.

After starting to write about the Doctor's life, I received a call
warning me not to write and not to publish this book as the Trust in
Switzerland is very powerful. My answer is: "History is a voice forever
sounding across the centuries, the laws of right and wrong. Opinions
alter, manners change, creeds rise and fall, but the moral law is written
on the tablets of eternity."

                                                Sigmund Freud

"If men could learn from history, what lessons it might teach us!
But passion and party blind our eyes, and the light, which experience

179

gives, is a lantern on the stern, which shines only on the waves behind us." Coleridge

The shadows we cast:

"The smallest bark on life's tumultuous ocean will leave a track behind for evermore; the slightest wave of influence set in motion extends and widens to the eternal shore." Miller

This is an excellent time to reflect upon the past, and the present, and to ponder the future. I just finished looking at the movie "'The Shoes of the Fisherman", 1968, staring Anthony Quinn as the Pope. The movie depicts the world in crisis, and Russia is asking the Pope for help. The Pope asks the question, "Why me, who am I, what have I learned?" While pondering these questions, the Chairman of the Trust called and outlined the new Trust program. The Trust has made a decision to abandon all other huge programs of industrialization and projects, and only concentrate on a medical field and food processing projects, which are basic projects for mankind. Now the Trust is asking me to study a basic plan for clinics that can be expanded to hospitals with phases as needed.

When I ask the question, "What have I learned?" I look back at years of building shopping centers, real estate management for Sears Roebuck and Company, being a developer for the General Services Administration in Detroit, Michigan, a consultant for Hilton Hotels management in Chicago, my development of the Samoset Resort in Maine, traveling throughout the Mideast, Eastern Europe, Africa and Asia, twelve to fourteen years of studies for the Trust, and being retooled to think as a European. Also, being the caregiver of two wives who died with cancer, and a hospice volunteer at the V.A. Hospital in Augusta, Maine, and now being 80 years of age, I still ask "What have I learned, who am I, and where am I going?". To try and answer these questions, and choose the right course, I read a book, <u>Making the Most of Your Life</u> by Jay R. Miller, published in 1891. In Chapter 6, he states, "It is never easy to become a scholar or to attain intellectual culture. It takes years and years of study and discipline to draw out and train the faculties of the mind. Intolerant, self-indulging students may have an easy time; he never troubles himself with difficult problems, he lets the hard things pass, not vexing his brain with them. But in evading the burden, he misses the blessings that were in it for him.

The only path to the joys and rewards of scholarship is that of patience, persistent toil. We cannot recover our treasures, the past will not give again its gold and pearls to any frantic appealing of ours. The dial of a clock in the palace of Napoleon at Malamaison, the maker put the words (non-nescitrevreti), it does not know how to go backwards. It is so with the great clock of time, it can never be turned backwards.

The moments come to us, but once whatever we do with them, we must do as they pass for they will never come to us again. These privileges make responsibility. We shall have to give account to God for all that He sends to us by the mystical hands of the passing hours and which we refuse or neglect to receive. They are wasted or are added to our debt. The real problem of living, therefore, is how to take what hours bring. He who does this will live nobly and faithfully, and will fulfill God's plan for his life. The difference in men is not in the opportunities that come to them, but in their use of these opportunities.

My window of opportunity is now closing, and to answer the question "Where am I going before the door closes?" is in God's hands, not mine. The future, the Trust, and all their noble ideals towards humanity is in the hands of God. There is never an answer to the great question of life and death, unless it is my answer or yours, because ultimately it is not a question that is answered, but a person. Our whole being has to be answered.

At that point, both question answers disappear like hunger after a good meal. God is subtle, but not malicious; we have to listen to the voices from the whirlwind as if its true meaning lay inside the logical framework of its words. We should notice how the answer consists mostly of questions (a good Jewish trait). The closest we can get to that question is: "What do we know?"

What the voice means is that paradise isn't situated in the past or future, and doesn't require a world tamed or edited by the normal sense. It is our world when we perceive it clearly. It is an experience of the Sabbath Vision, if we pay attention to the images themselves, we receive an attitude, not an argument. An attitude of "what is the righteous thing to do?" and that the righteous are not rewarded. We shall need our iron shoes if we are to make the journey of life that leads upward to the best possibilities of our life. Shoes of iron are promised only to those who are to have rugged roads, not to those whose path lies amid flowers.

In summary of my personal journey and stages of life, that I give thanks every day to Jesus that I have been given iron shoes to make the journey that leads to the best possibilities for my life.

Martin Olson

EPILOGUE

"The past is irreparable and irrevocable and it may seem idle to vex ourselves in thinking about doors now closed, that no tears, no prayers, no loud knocking can ever open again. Yes, yet the future remains. The years that are gone we cannot get back again, but new years are yet before us. They, too, will have their open doors. Shall we not learn wisdom as we look back upon the irrevocable past and make sure that in the future we shall not permit God's doors of opportunity to shut in our faces."

J.R. Miller, 1880

A world government for all the nations and all forms of religion, to open the doors of peace, no more wars, to sharply reduce the different forms of greed, and honesty by all its citizens so that all can have peace and enjoy God's gift of life.

Martin Olson